Mexican Folk Tales

TRANSLATED AND EDITED BY

Anthony John Campos

THE UNIVERSITY OF ARIZONA PRESS
TUCSON, ARIZONA

About the Editor . . .

ANTHONY JOHN CAMPOS, son of a Kansas-born father and a mother from the state of Jalisco in Mexico, grew up in a southern California barrio where many of the neighbors were also from Jalisco, and the folk culture was very much alive. He has traveled the world over and worked on the docks, in agriculture, as chicken-ranch hand, shoe salesman, cook, car salesman, and night watchman. Campos carried his interest in collecting folk tales to the University of California at Irvine, where he received a bachelor's degree in comparative culture in 1972, and to Norway, where in 1976 he began studying folklore at the University of Oslo and collecting Norwegian folk tales for a book. Working as a musician, he has developed local Norwegian tales into children's programs for Norsk Rikskringkasting, the Norwegian broadcasting system.

Copyright © 1977
The Arizona Board of Regents
All Rights Reserved
Manufactured in the U.S.A.

Library of Congress Cataloging in Publication Data
Mexican folk tales.
    1. Tales, Mexican — Mexico — Jalisco. I. Campos, Anthony John.
GR115.M45   398.2'0972'3   77-10603
ISBN 0-8165-0639-6
ISBN 0-8165-0560-8 pbk.

Mexican
Folk Tales

Illustrated by Mark Sanders

*To the innocent
children of
Vietnam*

Contents

THE FOIBLES OF MAN AND BEAST

Foreword

By setting down these Chicano legends — Mexican in origin, Indo-hispanic in character, but more recently part of the legends of the southwestern United States — Anthony John Campos enlarges and enriches the traditions of American literature. The assumption of these tales — that the moral imagination of a people may be disclosed through its myths and customs — is one shared by the major writers of North America, from Washington Irving to William Faulkner.

I first met Anthony Campos when he registered for a class I was teaching on contemporary Chicano literature at the University of California at Irvine. He had, it turned out, grown up on the Mexican tales his godmother Lily Cornejo loved to tell — the same ones that she had heard from her grandmother in Santa María, Jalisco, where she was born, and had heard retold as she and her father, who worked for the railroad, moved across the American Southwest in the early decades of this century. Anthony transcribed one of the tales, the one called "Juan Fetches the Devil," a story that has distinct affiliations not only with Mexican folklore, but with Spanish tales as far distant as the twelfth century. He then rendered the tale into English, and thereafter came to class regularly with new tales he had worked over and translated.

The tales stand by themselves, of course, but in back of them is the solid oral tradition of western European folk tales, and they are readily associable with certain recognized groupings. "San Pedro and Cristo" tales are widespread in Mexico and many European countries, and there is a large group of "Pedro de Ordinales" tales in the Spanish language. But, although the tradition of these stories is ultimately oral, now that they are written down, they show affiliations with other literary currents which have developed beyond the oral tradition.

Obviously, the tales have their most direct kinship with Mexican literature, particularly the *costumbrista* tradition of the portrayal of common life, including its cruel, miraculous, or diabolical aspects. This literary mode goes back to Francisco Bramón's *The Linnets of the Immaculate Virgin* (1620), but didn't become a powerful motive for fiction until the advent of nineteenth-century romanticism. At that time, the interest in local color and customs, the desire to explore the moral imagination of a people, and the recognition that the material environment, the land in particular, coincides roughly with the spiritual nature of the universe — these impulses and beliefs formed a distinct formula for the fictive imagination. Already coalescing in Fernández de Liardi's *El Periquillo Sarniento* (1816), and his play, *Auto Mariano to Commemorate the Miraculous Appearance of Our Mother and Lady of Guadalupe,* these tendencies came together in Manuel Payno's *El fistol del diablo* (1845–1846), which the author himself described as a "veritable depository, preserving the records and customs of the old Mexican society: its language, proverbs, styles of dress, conventions, tendencies." He described his later book, *The Bandits of Río Frío* (1889–1891), as a "naturalistic, humorous novel of customs, crimes and horrors."

Certainly there were to be later Mexican examples of this form, in collections of tales by Altamirano, Cuellar, Valle-Arizpe, and particularly by Lope Portillo y Rojas, the son of a prominent family of Jalisco, from whence the tales told by Anthony Campos also derive. As early as Payno, the interest in preserving the customs, language, proverbs, wisdom, mental habits, the humor, and the horrors of the old society are all brought together. However, the best late examples of this form are not, in fact, by Mexican writers, but by Domingo Faustino Sarmiento of Argentina in *Civilización y barbarie: Vida de Juan Facundo Quiroga* (1845), by Ricardo Palma of Peru in his ten volumes of *Tradiciones* (published between 1872 and 1910), and by Carlos Samayoa Chinchella of Guatemala in his tales of the *Popol Vuh.*

11

But Anthony Campos is neither a Mexican nor a South American writer; he once styled himself "a Chicano who writes in English." His Jalisco tales have in common the theme of the miraculous, in all its forms. The miracle story in its most obvious form, that involving a saint's intervention, occurs frequently. But the miraculous can also merge into a tale whose essence is its psychological realism, such as in "The Holy Child Visits a Prison." The devil himself, it turns out, in "The Devil Does a Good Deed," can even have good intentions and work miracles for those who treat him kindly. And man can also sometimes work a miracle and get into heaven by tricking St. Peter, as in "Pedro de Ordinales Goes to Heaven."

Still, there is no conventional morality. On the contrary, there is the recognition that virtue may not always be rewarded but quite the reverse, as in "A Reward for Honesty." And ultimately, there is a skepticism about specific miracles, which is best summarized in the conclusion of "The Reason for Turtles": "That is why we have turtles today. . . . They say, anyway, that this is why we have turtles. If you think about it, it seems right — maybe it is."

Miracles might be questioned, but there is no doubting the belief in the miraculous which is present in the tales. The daily, the commonplace, the quotidian, indeed all of life, are regarded with wonder, and yet with a calm acceptance of the inexplicable. The sense of the miraculous, understood as natural and inevitable, is, in the end, a radiation of the essential quality of the tales — an affection for life and the living, and an assumption that life originates from and fulfills itself in goodness.

The ghostly voices of rural Jalisco and the whispers of those itinerant workers of the Southwest who were driven north by the revolution linger in the tales, and are given voice once again by Anthony John Campos in his English rendition.

JAY MARTIN

A Word
From the Editor

These tales were told to me in Spanish by my godmother, Lily Cornejo. As a young girl, she had heard them from her grandmother, Mama Nella, and memorized them. They were recounted with the archaic words and colloquial usages of rural Jalisco still embedded in them. I remember also my godmother telling me how all the children in the family would sit around an oil lamp, drinking coffee and listening to Mama Nella telling these stories. Years later, I myself sat at a dinner table and listened to them retold by my godmother.

The stories became an integral part of our family's moral and religious education. If my godmother wanted to make a moral point against vaingloriousness, she would remind us of the fate of the hermit in the tale, "The Priest Goes Down to Hell." If it was against being naive or foolish, she would point out the fate of the peasant in the tale, "A Reward for Honesty."

Man, as is brought out in the tales, is the trickster: in his quest for money and possessions, he commits all crimes, from murdering his best friend to selling the soul of his son. Contrarily, the Devil — whether indirectly saving the soul of Abrilio in the tale, "The Priest Goes Down to Hell," or directly — by summoning a priest to administer the last rites to the dying old lady in "The Devil Does a Good Deed" — acts with honor. I recall my godmother's words, "Nowadays, the people are worse devils than the Devil himself."

For some years I harbored the idea of putting these tales in writing, and when I finally began working on the project, it turned into a family enterprise as we sat around the dinner table at my grandfather's home. If my godmother forgot some incident from a tale, my mother, who had also listened to Mama Nella as a child, would remind her. I tape-recorded the tales in Spanish and reworked them into English.

I would like to express my thanks to Professor Jay Martin who helped arrange the tales in their present book form and through whose efforts they were brought to the University of Arizona Press. Gratitude is also due to the University of Arizona Press for effecting their publication.

A. J. C.

LEGENDS

OF THE DEVIL

Juan Fetches the Devil

THERE was an old man and woman and they had a son called Juan. Juan had such an insatiable appetite that he was eating them out of the home and toward the hill. They had arrived at a point where despair and hunger were overwhelming them.

One evening, after they had finished their meager supper, they asked, "Juan, why don't you go fetch the devil and bring him here?"

Juan didn't answer because he was very sad. He went to his room to get some sleep. He sat on his bed and began thinking, "Sure, I'll go fetch him. My mother and father want me to fetch the devil, so I'll go do it." And away he went, walking and walking and eating what got in his way.

He continued walking until he came to a cliff that overlooked the wide ocean. He began conversing with an old man who was sitting on the cliff. "Sir, I'm looking for the devil. Can you give me some idea where I can find him?"

The old man thought for a moment. "I've heard people say that he lives across the water on the other side. There's a large cave where fire comes out, and that must be his home."

"How am I going to cross the ocean?" Juan asked the old man.

"There's an eagle that will take you across on his back," the old man said. "But you will have to furnish seven cows because he has such an enormous appetite that every time he cries out for meat, you will have to feed him one of the cows."

So, Juan went and stole the cows from a nearby ranch. Then he went to where the eagle's nest was and asked him to carry him across the water. The eagle agreed, and soon they were flying high over the ocean.

They had flown only a short way when Juan, who was on the back of the eagle along with the seven cows, heard "Meat, I want meat." So he threw down one of the cows and the eagle quickly devoured it.

When they had flown a bit further over the ocean, Juan heard the eagle crying out again, "Meat, I want more meat." Once again, Juan threw a cow to the hungry eagle.

By this time Juan was also getting very hungry and the eagle kept eating cow after cow. Juan finally said to the eagle, "Well, it seems that you want to eat everything and don't want to leave anything for me."

"Shut up, or I'm going to eat you," said the eagle.

"What's that?" cried Juan. "Before you eat me, I'll eat you."

As soon as Juan said this, the eagle turned over backwards and Juan went spinning down into the ocean. Fortunately for him, he fell near land and was able to swim to shore.

When he was on dry land again, Juan began asking the people he met, "Where is the cave that has fire coming out of it?" They told him that the cave was located in the middle of a large desert that was very far away. So Juan started walking and he walked for miles and miles.

When it began to get dark, he became very hungry and started looking around for something to eat. He saw a coyote and started running after him until he caught him by the tail.

"I'm going to eat you," said Juan to the coyote.

"Please don't eat me," said the coyote. "I know the whole desert and I'll take you to whatever place you're looking for."

Juan thought about it for awhile and finally said, "I'm looking for a cave that has fire coming out of it. Can you take me there?"

"I know where that cave is," said the coyote, "but it will take three days to get there."

Juan got on the back of the coyote and off they went into the wilderness. When they had traveled a whole day, Juan was so hungry that he was ready to eat the coyote.

"Please don't eat me," said the coyote. "There's a friend of mine that lives near by. You can eat there."

So, off they went till they came to a cave where a bear lived.

"What do you have to eat?" Juan asked the bear.

"Nothing at all," said the bear.

"Well, then, I'm going to eat you," said Juan, and he gulped down the poor bear.

Juan and the coyote went to sleep, and the next morning they started on the road again. When it started to get dark, Juan began to get very hungry and said to the coyote, "I'm so hungry that I can't stand it anymore. I'm going to eat you."

The coyote said, "Please don't eat me. I know a friend where we can get some food."

So, they went to a cave where a wolf lived.

"What do you have to eat?" Juan asked the wolf.

"Nothing," answered the wolf.

"Well, I'm going to eat you," said Juan.

After he had eaten the wolf, Juan and the coyote went to sleep.

The next morning, bright and early, Juan and the coyote went on their way again. When it started getting late, Juan was very hungry and said to the coyote, "I'm so hungry that I'm going to eat you."

"Please don't eat me," said the coyote. "I know a friend where we can get something to eat."

So, off they went.

It was getting pretty late in the evening, and it was dark when they came to the cave.

"Knock on the door," said the coyote, and he gave Juan a pair of pliers. "When he puts his head out the door, you grab him by the nose."

Juan knocked, but nobody answered.

"Just take a peek so you can see who it is that's knocking," said Juan.

The door opened and Juan took the pliers, grabbed the nose, and pulled. Out popped the devil himself!

"What do you want with me?" asked the devil.

Juan told him the whole story of how his parents had sent him. He then told the devil to fly him home, and off they went with Juan holding him by the nose.

When they got to Juan's house, his mother and father said, "Who is this?"

"It's the devil," Juan answered. "You told me to fetch the devil, and here he is."

Juan's parents were very frightened and asked Juan to forgive them.

The devil then went and fetched the coyote and said, "Every time you get hungry, you pluck a hair from the coyote's tail and it will then turn into a cow. From now on, all of you will have enough to eat."

So, the devil flew off into the starry night, and Juan, his parents, and the coyote all sat down to dinner and coffee.

The Rich Ranchero's Maguey Fence

NEAR Rangel, there lived a rich ranchero. Not being satisfied with the wealth he had been born into, he had added more parcels of property to the already vast hacienda. Over the years, he had accumulated over one hundred peons and his property had grown so large that it took a man on horseback a day and a half to cross from one end to the other.

Morning and evening this rich ranchero could be seen riding from one valley to the next, stopping here and there to talk to the vaqueros tending his herds. Being a pensive man and aided by the region's remoteness, he would sink into deep contemplation as he made his way on horseback. After much of such contemplation, he decided to build a fence that would encircle his entire property. He wanted the fence built of magueys with a six-foot deep moat running alongside.

One evening he was riding along in a remote part of his hacienda. All his vast territory was visible to him from the high mesa where he stood. "I would give anything I own to have the moat dug and the magueys planted," he thought to himself. But he was aware that, in spite of his immense wealth, so great a task was beyond his means. He continued on until he came to where a grove of cacti stood. He got off his horse, lay himself in the shade to rest, and was soon fast asleep.

The ranchero had been sleeping for some time when he was awakened by the strong smell of sulphur. The first thing he noticed was two feet, one of a cock and one of a mule. As his glance went higher, he saw that they were the feet of a tall man wearing a long cape. "This is certainly the devil," he said to himself.

The ranchero got up and explained his situation to the devil. He said that he wanted his land fenced and asked the devil to assist him.

The devil said, "What will you give me in exchange for putting up your fence?"

"I have buried three brass caskets filled with gold," replied the ranchero. "All three will be yours when the job is finished."

"We make all the gold where I come from so I don't need your gold," the devil answered. "But I'll tell you what. You don't need to give me anything during your lifetime. But after your death, I will take your soul. Is that agreeable with you?"

The ranchero liked the idea of having his land fenced, but not of selling his soul. "Meet me here tomorrow evening and I shall give you a reply," he told the devil. He went home and pondered his problem until the wee hours of the morning. Finally, he thought of a solution.

The following evening he rode off to the site where he was to meet the devil. He had a cock and a piece of mirror concealed under his cloak. When the devil appeared the ranchero said to him, "If you finish the fence before the cock crows, you shall have my soul. But if you don't finish, then I shall keep the fence and my soul."

"Fair enough," said the devil.

The devil summoned a crew of his minions and they began working with such tremendous speed, they were like a ray of lightning. The ranchero kept digging his spurs into his horse, making him go faster and faster to stay ahead of the devil and his crew. But the workers threw the magueys into place so fast that several times they nearly trampled over him.

On and on into the dark night rode the ranchero, the devil and his crew always hot on his heels. So great were the workers' efforts that the noise could be heard for miles around. It seemed as if all the condemned in hell were there building the ranchero's maguey fence.

When his horse was about to collapse from exhaustion, the ranchero noticed that he was almost back to the beginning of the line of magueys and the moat where the devil had begun building. The devil also noticed that he had gone full circle and was about to complete the fence, and he tortured his minions into going faster than ever.

The desperate ranchero pulled his cock out and began slapping him in the head. The devil and his crew were almost finished when he finally succeeded in waking the unhappy cock. The ranchero took the mirror out from under his cloak and placed it in front of the cock. When the cock saw his reflection in the mirror, he began to crow loudly. When the ranchero turned to look back, he heard a loud noise and saw a large ball of fire where the devil had been a few moments before. The ranchero got off his horse and started walking home in the twilight.

My grandfather says the ranchero often tried to complete the unfinished fence but was unable to as something would always happen. Either the magueys dried up or they would disappear altogether.

The fence remains unfinished to this very day.

The Devil
Does a Good Deed

THERE was an old lady who lived all alone on a small ranch. The ranch was in the middle of a large desert and, because of its remoteness, very few people traveled there. Perhaps, once or twice a year, a muleteer would take a wrong turn and come across the ranch by accident. That was the only time the old lady received news from the outside world.

She had been living in this manner since the death of her husband, who had belonged to a gang of bandits. The leader of this band was a notoriously infamous rascal who was feared throughout the territory. After one dangerous raid, in which they had encountered federal troops, the leader had given her husband a painting of a devil, as a token of gratitude for saving his life during the encounter. When the husband saw what it was, he did not want to accept it. However, he could not refuse a gift from a friend.

When he had arrived home, the husband had placed the picture behind a door, and there it had stayed. As the old lady went about her daily chores, she would come to the door where the painting was hanging and say, "Poor you, who never sees the face of God." She would then take her broom and swat the dust off. This daily ritual went on for many years.

There came a time when the old lady became very ill. She tried to take care of herself as best she could and prepared all the remedies she knew, but to no avail. She grew weaker and weaker day by day. Finally, she just lay in bed and was unable to move.

When the devil saw the condition she was in, he went up to her bed. The old lady knew that death was near. "Good-bye, old friend," she said to the devil. When the devil heard this, he rushed out of the house as fast as he could and started running down the street toward the nearest town.

When he came to the town, he went inside the first church he could find. When the priest saw the devil, he recoiled away. "What do you want here?" asked the priest.

"I want you to come with me and administer the last sacrament to someone who is dying," said the devil.

When the priest heard this, he understood. They hitched the horses to the priest's carriage and rode off in the direction of the old lady's ranch.

When they finally came to the ranch, they found the old lady smiling. "I saw a beautiful lady dressed in white," she whispered. "She was coming down a long tunnel and little boys with wings were flying all around."

The priest confessed the old lady, and she died peacefully. The priest then told the devil to leave, and he himself started back toward his church.

And so, I suppose the devil was gone before the gravediggers came to put the old lady under the ground.

The Pulque Vendor
Tricks the Devil

NEAR Guadalajara, there once lived a pulque*
vendor. In one street and out the other, swerving
and swaying to his heart's delight, he went along
his way. People were so accustomed to his daily route
that for many years the high falsetto yell that announced
his presence was used as a means of telling time. "Here
comes the pulque vendor," they would cry.

This gentleman had taken it into his head to build
a bridge across the river. He chose a site near a grove
of cacti and drew a plan of the bridge. But when he had
finished the plan, he realized that he did not have
enough money to carry out his idea. In spite of this, he
did not lose heart but continued to earn whatever money
he could by selling his pulque.

---

*Fermented juice of the maguey.

One evening, he was walking along the river toward the spot where the grove of cacti stood. It was a pleasantly fresh evening with occasional warm breezes that scattered the scent of flowers through the streets. The pulque vendor had worked hard all day and now abandoned himself to thought. "After all these years of sacrifice, I still don't have enough money to build the bridge," he lamented. He knew that he did not have many years left to live.

He finally arrived at the site where the bridge was to be built. But unlike countless other evenings when he had been there, he noticed the figure of a tall man wearing a black cloak. After they had exchanged greetings, the stranger asked, "What will you give me in exchange for building the bridge across the river?"

"All I can offer you is the money that I have saved and some pulque that's inside my cart," replied the vendor.

"Will you go with me if I finish building the bridge before daybreak?" the stranger asked.

"No, I will not promise you anything like that," replied the vendor.

"Very well," said the devil. "Then how about this. If the cock crows before I have completed the bridge, you need not go with me."

On these new terms the vendor agreed, for he thought his chances much better. After all, a cock might crow at any time during the night, and one was almost certain to crow before daybreak.

The vendor sat down on the river bank and watched as the devil began his task. "My bridge will finally be built after all these years," he thought. His confidence was so great that he even decided to take a nap.

While the vendor slept, the devil worked feverishly, putting brick after brick into place until soon the whole foundation was laid. The effort he made was so great that all his clothes were soaked with perspiration. Soon he had accumulated a great thirst, but still he continued working.

When the vendor awoke, he rubbed his eyes and looked toward the river. He was astonished at the progress the devil had made. The whole bridge was complete except for one last tower that the devil was now working on. The vendor became very anxious for it was almost daybreak and not a single cock had crowed. "What shall I do?" he wondered. "What will become of me if the wretched cocks fail to crow before the devil completes the tower?"

By this time, the devil was down to his last few bricks. "I have almost finished my work and you must soon go away with me," he laughed.

"Yes, I will go with you," answered the vendor, "but let's drink a toast to your victory."

Seeing that only one brick remained to be placed, the devil agreed. "There's no way I can possibly lose now, and besides, I'm dying of thirst," he thought.

The vendor pulled his cart over to where the devil was standing. "I have two kinds of pulque in my cart," said the vendor. "One is called 'El que se queda' and the other, 'El que se va.'* Which do you prefer?"

"I'll take 'el que se queda,'" replied the devil. "In honor of my bridge that will remain here on earth. But you can drink 'el que se va' because you will soon be long gone." The devil began laughing.

The vendor found the two largest glasses he had and filled them to overflowing. The devil was so thirsty that he emptied his glass in one gulp.

"Have another glass," said the vendor.

The devil took the second glass, but he passed out on the ground before he finished it. Just then a burst of sunlight opened up the sky, and the crowing of a cock was heard in the distance.

The devil, who was still lying on the ground, suddenly burst into a ball of flame and disappeared. The drink was too strong, even for the devil. It wasn't called "el que se queda" without reason.

To this day, nobody has ever been able to finish the bridge. Many people have put the last brick into place, but when they come to see it the next morning, it has fallen off or disappeared.

---

*The one which stays and the one which goes.

The Priest
Goes Down to Hell

ONCE upon a time there was a husband and wife who were very, very poor. They had been married for many years, but had no children. Since they were both quite old, they had given up hope of having a child. But still the wife would go off alone to pray to the Lord saying, "Please send us a son so that our old age will not seem so lonely."

One day the husband finally became desperate and said to his wife, "I'm fed up with being poor. I'm going to see where I can find some money. If I meet the devil, I'll ask the devil for money." And off he went.

He had walked just a short way when he met the devil on the corner. The devil asked, "Where are you going, my good man?"

"I'm looking for the devil," replied the man. "I'm tired of being poor and if asking the devil is the only way of getting money, that's how it has to be."

"I'm the devil," said the stranger. "If I give you the money, what will you give me in return?" The man thought to himself, "When will I have a son? I never will." He was certain of this fact.

"What will you give me in exchange for money?" repeated the devil.

The man said, "My son's soul — the first son that I have."

The devil agreed, and they made a contract and signed it in blood.

When they were finished signing, the devil said, "Look, there's a big rock behind that mesquite tree. Lift it up and take all the money you want. Whenever you need money, it will be there."

The man began to buy ranches with the money and was soon one of the richest men in the region.

A short time went by and the man and wife were becoming used to their new life of prosperity. They now had maids who cleaned the house and servants who prepared their meals. One evening, when they had finished supper, the wife said to her husband, "I have something to tell you, a surprise."

"Well, what is it?" asked the husband.

"I'm pregnant, and soon we shall have a son," the wife beamed.

The husband was shocked by this news, but didn't say anything to his wife.

A few months later, a son was born. He was a beautiful baby. When the father saw the child, he became very sad. His wife could not understand the reason for his unhappiness. "After all these years of prayer, we finally have a son," she told her husband.

As the child grew older, the woman noticed that her husband became even sadder. When the child was four or five years old, he began to go to school. He was a very bright boy and by the time he was ten, he was already very learned. He was given the best education that money could buy.

When he grew even older, the boy decided to become a priest and when he turned eighteen, he went away to the seminary. But whenever he came home, he noticed that his father shied away from him. The father's eyes would fill with tears and he would go down to the cellar and lock himself away.

The boy also became very sad on these occasions. "Doesn't my father love me?" he would ask his mother. "If he doesn't want me to come home anymore, why doesn't he tell me? I have never offended him. Why doesn't he like me?"

The woman would then go to her husband and ask, "What's wrong with you? Our son is sad every time he comes home. He says that you don't want to see him or eat with him." The man would tell his wife that nothing was wrong and would go up to his room.

Several years passed by and the time came for the boy to be ordained a priest. He loved his parents dearly and wanted them both to come to the ceremony, but his father had constructed a large cellar in which to hide when his son came home and went there instead. When the young man finally arrived home, he told his mother that he wanted to have a talk with his father.

"Where is he?" he asked. "I want to see him now."

After much pleading, the woman finally told her son where his father was. The son went down to where his father was hiding and started talking to him.

"If you don't want me to come home anymore, I won't. But please tell me the reason why," he said.

His father then began to weep bitterly. He told his son how he had made the contract with the devil for his soul. "Forgive me," he said. "Your mother and I were very old and had never been able to have a son. Your birth was the last thing that I expected to happen."

The son then understood why his father had acted so strangely whenever they met. He told his father that he was going to search for the devil.

"Give me a team of mules, servants, and some provisions," he said.

"Where are you going to look for the devil?" asked his father.

"I don't know, but I'll find him somewhere," the son assured him.

Early the next morning, the priest left with his servants and began walking and walking. After seven days of traveling, when they were deep inside a desert, they happened to meet a hermit. The hermit told the priest that he had been in the desert for ten years. The priest then told the hermit his story.

"Señor, we are on a mission. After so many years in the desert, do you know where the devil lives?"

"No, my son," replied the hermit. "Even after serving God all these years, I still don't know. But further down there is another hermit who has been serving God for twenty years. Maybe he can help you."

Early the next morning, the priest and his group started walking in the desert again. After they had traveled several hours, they came to a cave on the side of a hill. The priest looked into the dark cave and saw a fire burning.

"This must be the second hermit's home," he said.

He walked up to the fire and saw a man sitting there. He asked the hermit if he knew where the devil lived.

"I've been here for many years, but I have never come to know where the devil lives," replied the hermit. "But, further down there is a hermit who has been in the desert serving God for thirty years. Perhaps he will help you."

The priest and his servants made their camp and spent the night in the cave.

Early the next morning, they started walking in the desert again. It was extremely hot and the sun was directly overhead, beating down on them. They took shelter at the foot of a mountain stream. Everyone was resting and the animals were drinking water. Suddenly they heard a loud flutter, and when they looked up, they saw an angel flying away in the distance.

"That must be the place where the third hermit lives," said the priest.

He started walking toward the place where he had

seen the angel. When he got there, he saw a hermit eating. Never in his life had the priest seen such splendid dishes.

"Who are you?" asked the hermit.

"I am a priest on a mission to find the devil. Perhaps you can tell me where I can find him," said the son.

"I have been in the desert for many, many years, but I still don't know where the devil lives," replied the hermit. "But, further down there lives a bandit called Abrilio. He is so mean and treacherous that the devil himself has made him his compadre. The devil takes him down to hell three times a day."

When the priest heard this news he was overjoyed and he slept peacefully that night.

Early the next morning, the priest and his group began walking again. When it was almost dark, they came to the ranch where Abrilio's bandits were hiding. When the bandits saw them, they started to attack them. Fortunately, Abrilio was watching and told his men to let them enter. The priest, who was dressed in lay clothing, went up to where Abrilio was standing.

"Señor," he said, "I am here on a mission looking for the devil. Do you happen to know where I can find him?"

"Of course," replied Abrilio. "He's my compadre and won't be long in coming."

He told the priest to make himself at home and ordered his men to feed and water the mules. "Be careful not to steal anything," he warned his men. They sat down to talk and afterwards they all went to sleep.

Around midnight the priest was awakened by a frightful noise. He stood up and noticed the devil standing in the doorway. When the devil saw the priest, he didn't want to come inside.

"Come inside, compadre," Abrilio told the devil. The devil was still reluctant to enter. "This young man is looking for someone who will take him down to hell," insisted Abrilio. "I told him that we were compadres. Maybe you can help him."

The devil finally agreed. "I'll take him," he said. "If he really wants to go, I'll take him."

The devil told the priest to climb on his shoulders. "You must not open your eyes no matter what you hear," warned the devil, "or you will remain in the void."

Soon they were going through the air. The sounds of music and merriment reached the priest's ears, and he was tempted to open his eyes.

"Are we there yet?" he asked.

"We're not very far off," replied the devil. "We'll be there right away."

"You can open your eyes now," the devil said when they had arrived. As soon as the other devils saw the priest, they all left. Lucifer was the only one that remained.

"Why have you brought him here?" demanded Lucifer.

The devil told him that he was looking for a contract that another one of the devils had made years ago.

"Which devil has the contract?" Lucifer asked.

The priest told him his father had made the contract and that he didn't know.

Lucifer then sent for all the devils that were traveling in the world. As the devils arrived, they were tortured. They were whipped. They were made to drink molten lead. And they were thrown in the furnaces. But all to no avail. Not one of them had the contract.

When it was almost dawn and they were about ready to give up, Lucifer said, "There's one devil left, el diablo cojo.* He's the one that brings me the most souls." They sat down to wait for him.

They had not been waiting long when the last devil arrived. Lucifer called him over.

"What do you want with me?" asked el diablo cojo.

Lucifer told him that they had searched everyone and still hadn't found the contract. "You must have it on you," said Lucifer.

"I don't have the contract," insisted el diablo cojo.

Lucifer then gave orders for him to be tortured. They did the most horrible things imaginable to him. They made him drink molten lead. They made him walk on spikes. And they threw him in the furnace. But all to no avail. He didn't turn over the contract.

"All right," said Lucifer. "If he doesn't want to turn it over, then throw him into Abrilio's bed."

When el diablo cojo heard this he said, "I won't get into Abrilio's bed." He then opened up his crooked leg and took out the contract.

———————————

*The lame one.

Lucifer gave the contract to the priest and told the devil to take him back to earth. The devil told the priest to get on his shoulders and do the same as before. They flew off and were soon back at Abrilio's ranch.

When they arrived, the priest climbed off the devil's shoulders. "You can go back now," he told the devil.

When Abrilio saw the priest, he was very curious to know what had happened. He always went to hell with his compadre but was used to an elegant place with dancing, lively music, and merriment. "Tell me what happened," said Abrilio.

The priest then told Abrilio all about his trip. "It was such a problem to find the contract. They tortured all the devils until there remained only one. They tortured him also, but he still didn't want to turn over the contract. Finally, Lucifer threatened to throw him in the bed of one called Abrilio. As soon as el diablo cojo heard this, he opened his crooked leg and turned over the contract."

Abrilio listened in silence, then became pale and fell to his knees. "Father, confess me," he pleaded. "If even the devil did not want my bed, how horrible it must be." As soon as he said this, he fell dead at the priest's feet.

The hermit, who ate from the hand of God, was starving to death. He would come out of his cave and look up at the sky and say, "What are you doing, angel of God? Can't you see I'm dying of hunger?"

Finally, after three days without food, he saw the angel coming. "Where were you, angel of God? I almost died of hunger."

"Who would have remembered?" replied the angel. "We were having a great feast and celebrating."

"Who died?" asked the hermit. "A cardinal? A Bishop? Or did the Pope die?"

"Nothing of the kind," answered the angel. "Something much greater than that. The soul of Abrilio was saved."

"What?" said the surprised hermit. "If they gave Abrilio, who was the devil's compadre, such a great feast, imagine what it will be like when I finally die."

For speaking these words, the hermit found himself in Abrilio's bed instead of going to heaven. That's why they say that it's not good to be vainglorious in this world.

THE STRANGE DOINGS
OF THE SAINTS

Señor San Antonio Retrieves an Axe

IT was the feast day of Señor San Antonio and groups of children were going around singing from house to house. One of the groups, that was on its way back from a distant rancho, suddenly remembered that an old lady lived nearby.

"Let's pay her a visit," one of the children suggested. "She must be very lonely all by herself."

The group started up the road that led to the old lady's house.

The old lady and her husband had not been blessed with any children. Consequently, when her husband died, the old lady was left alone, or so it seemed. Her neighbors had been very concerned at first but they soon got used to seeing her perform even the hardest chores. People were often amazed at her large piles of

47

firewood. "She must have the strength of three men," they whispered.

As the group of children approached the old lady's house, they heard an excited voice scolding someone inside. "You rascal! You ought to be ashamed. Why do I need you if you don't take care of me?" she cried. "See — they've stolen my axe. Now how am I going to chop wood? You're the only man I have around, and you don't take care of me," she went on and on.

The youngsters were bewildered by what they heard and were curious to find out who the old lady was talking to. When they peeped in the window, they saw her talking to an old picture of Señor San Antonio hanging on the wall. The old lady was so occupied that she didn't even notice the children.

The children stood around for awhile, watching Señor San Antonio get bawled out. Finally, one of them knocked on the door and the old lady invited them in. She soon fell captive to the festive atmosphere that the singers brought and forgot all about her stolen axe. The old lady made some atole* and the children continued singing until it got late and they had to go home.

A few miles away, the thief was admiring the axe he had acquired. "What a fine axe. It will certainly come in handy," he thought. He was very tired and soon fell fast asleep.

The next morning was extremely cold and the thief decided to warm up his sluggish body by chopping some

---

*Mexican drink made with cornmeal.

wood. "This is as good a time as any to try out my new axe," he said, shivering.

There was a mesquite trunk a short distance from the campsite. The thief got the axe, walked over to the trunk, took a deep breath, and delivered a mighty blow. The force of the impact sent splinters flying in all directions and one of them lodged in his eye. He began swearing and became so angry that he left without having breakfast.

The rest of the morning went by very quickly. The thief, who had not eaten since the previous evening, was very hungry. He stopped his horse by a bridge and started looking for firewood. He found a log embedded in the ground near the river and went to get the axe from his horse. He walked up to the log, planted his feet, aimed his axe, and delivered a crashing blow. The blade slipped and the blunt end of the axe went sliding down the slippery log — right into his ankle bone. The thief fell to the ground clutching his ankle. He was in so much pain that he even forgot to curse.

The thief was still lying on the ground recovering from the pain when he heard footsteps creaking on the bridge. A man on a burro had crossed over from the other side of the river.

"Are you all right?" the man called down to him.

The thief answered that he was.

The two men began talking and were soon deep in conversation. The man on the burro said that he lived on a ranch a half-day's ride ahead. He said he was hungry and asked to borrow the axe to chop some firewood.

The stranger went up to the log and began chopping away effortlessly. Soon he had a large pile of firewood ready. The thief could not believe his eyes.

"Let me have that axe for a minute," he cried.

He took the axe, planted his feet firmly, and took a big swing. A large piece of wood went flying through the air and hit him right on the head.

"You cursed axe," he screamed and hurled it with all his strength into the river.

The old lady was busy spinning wool on her spinning wheel. She was daydreaming about heaven knows what. Everything was so peaceful and quiet that the gentle hum of the spinning wheel was putting her to sleep. Suddenly her daydream was shattered into a thousand pieces. The axe came hurtling through the window.

"You've brought it back," cried the old lady to Señor San Antonio. "You see, you're afraid of me."

Pedro de Ordinales
Goes to Heaven

PEDRO de Ordinales was a shepherd and spent most of his time in the mountains with his sheep and dogs. He only went into town twice a year to buy provisions. To avoid being lonely, he daydreamed his time away.

"They say that there is a heaven and a hell," he thought. "More than anything in the world, I would like to find out where they are."

As the months went by Pedro found himself thinking of heaven and hell more and more. Finally, when he could stand it no longer, he asked his brother to tend his sheep and he began walking down a dirt road. He continued walking until he came to a place where the road split in three directions.

"Which way shall I go?" Pedro wondered as he rested by the side of the road.

51

He finally began walking down the road that led to the left. He had not gone very far when he began hearing horrible noises. "I don't like it here," he thought and ran back to the crossing.

When he got back he decided to take the road that went toward the right. He walked and walked. When he had walked for about an hour, he began catching the strong smell of sulphur. "Oh, oh," he cried. "This road must certainly lead to the devil." And he went back to the crossing again.

This time he took the last road, which was the middle one, and began walking again. He walked until he came to a big golden gate. "This must be the gate to heaven," he thought. "If only there were a way for me to get in."

Pedro finally decided to knock. He knocked and knocked and was about to give up when he heard someone shout, "Who is it?"

"It's me," Pedro quickly replied.

"Who's me?" answered the voice.

"Open up a bit and you'll see who it is," cried Pedro de Ordinales.

St. Peter thought for a moment. "It won't hurt to take a look," he finally decided because he was curious to see who it was. He picked up his keys, walked to the gate, and opened the door a tiny bit, just enough to peek with one eye.

When Pedro de Ordinales saw the opening, he quickly put his finger into the crack. When St. Peter saw this, he slammed the door on Pedro's finger.

"Ay, ay, ay, tocayito*," Pedro screamed. "Please open up a bit so that I can get my finger out."

"I'll open up a bit just to get rid of him," thought St. Peter.

He opened the door a little bit more. When Pedro felt the pressure loosen on his finger, he shoved his whole hand inside. St. Peter quickly shut the door again.

"Tocayito, tocayito," Pedro pleaded. "I was about to take my hand out when you closed it again."

God the Father was sleeping nearby. St. Peter could hear his snoring from where he stood. "I wish I could get rid of this nuisance," he said to himself. He was afraid that Pedro, who was raising such a big commotion, might wake up God the Father.

"I'm going to loosen the door," he said to Pedro. "Then you pull your hand out and go away."

As soon as Pedro felt the door loosen, he pushed as hard as he could. He pushed so hard that St. Peter was sent sprawling and Pedro landed on top of him.

"What are you doing, you crazy man?" St. Peter shouted.

They both got up and began to argue loudly. God the Father, who had been awakened from a beautiful dream, came rushing over to where they were standing.

"What's happening?" he stormed. "Who is this man?"

St. Peter explained what had happened. "He forced his way in, Sir."

---

*Little friend.

When God the Father heard this, he walked over to Pedro. "You will be turned into a stone," he cried.

Pedro thought for a moment, then said, "Si Señor, but with eyes."

Pedro, the shepherd, was then transformed into a rock. He is lying there at heaven's gate now and can see everything that's going on. But he never moves. That is, unless some passerby kicks him.

A Farmer
Learns a Lesson

THERE were three brothers who were born on a farm in Mexico and grew up to be strong young men. The two younger brothers were very close and always did things together. If you saw one of them, you could be sure that the other was nearby. The oldest brother felt very left out and grew up to be resentful and bitter.

When the father died, he left a plot of land to each of the brothers. The oldest brother had expected to receive all of his father's property and when he found out that he had to share equally with his brothers, he grew more resentful than ever.

When planting time came, the three brothers went out to work their fields. The land was very arid and this made the soil difficult to till.

The two younger brothers took it in stride. "God wants it so," they said and continued their labor.

However, their older brother was in a rage. "How miserable I am," he cried and began to hurl blasphemous insults at God and the saints.

One morning, a man on a burro came riding toward the brothers. Not many strangers passed by their farm since it was located in a very remote area. When the man on the burro got near, they stopped their tilling to have a closer look.

The man was bearded and had long flowing hair that fell to his shoulders. He said he had been traveling for many hours and was very thirsty. The youngest son ran to the well and fetched some water. The bearded man sat down and drank the water.

"What are you planting?" he asked.

"Barley, sir," answered the young man.

"Barley shall you reap, my son," he said.

He got on his burro and started down the road. He stopped when he came to where the second brother was working.

"Good day," the brother said. "Where do you come from?"

"I come from a distant kingdom," replied the stranger. "What are you growing, my son?"

"Wheat, sir," answered the young man.

"Wheat shall you reap, my son," answered the bearded man.

He stayed for a while with the second brother, then started on his way. When he came to the oldest brother, he stopped and got off his burro again.

"What are you planting, my son?" asked the stranger.

"Rocks," growled the embittered man.

"Rocks shall you reap," said the stranger and left. The oldest son just sneered at him and continued with his work.

When harvest time came around, the two younger brothers were busy gathering their abundant crops. Never before had anyone grown such fine crops and people came from all over the region to see them.

The oldest brother, however, was in a state of desperation. All of his fields were covered with rocks — nothing but rocks of all sizes and shapes.

When the younger brothers saw his plight, they went up and comforted him. He was deeply moved by their gesture.

"I will never again be mean to my fellow man," he cried. "I have learned a good lesson. From this day on, whenever I look at a rock it will serve as a reminder that what you sow in life, so shall you reap."

The Woman Who Was Saved by a Miracle

THERE was a couple who lived in a small town. The woman was very beautiful and as a result, received many compliments from young rancheros as she walked down the street. Her husband, an adobe maker, was very jealous and had been planning to kill her for quite some time.

One night, instead of coming right home from work, he headed for the cantina. He got very drunk and began talking with a tall stranger sitting next to him. The bearded man said he was a traveling salesman and sold statues of the saints and crucifixes. He told how he had traveled to distant parts of Mexico and made many friends. After some time the stranger excused himself, saying he was tired and wanted to go to bed. The adobe maker had a few more drinks and went home.

When he got there, his wife greeted him happily at the door. She told her husband that she had a surprise in the next room. When the woman led him to the new crucifix hanging on the wall, he began to rave in a drunken stupor. He went into the next room and hid a dagger under his vest.

The woman went to bed as usual. She had waited up for her husband and it was now very late at night. She blew out the candle and went to sleep peacefully. By this time her husband had worked himself into a fury. As the woman dreamed, he leaped on top of her and plunged the dagger into her heart three times. Her blood flowed and she screamed agonizingly and died.

The woman's screams broke the silence of the starry night. Many who heard them crossed themselves. Some thought it was an animal out in the brush, and others that it was drunks arguing. The man got very scared and ran out of the house to a small hill nearby. He watched his house intently to see if anyone came, keeping up his vigil the entire night. Before he knew it, the cocks were singing and the morning had broken.

The man grew very remorseful. He realized that he had not been having a terrible nightmare, but had actually committed a wicked murder.

"What have I done?" he cried. "I have killed the most gentle woman in the whole world."

Suddenly he remembered that for years his wife had gotten up at dawn each morning to go to early mass. When he glanced down, he saw somebody coming out of his house — a woman wearing a shawl.

"Who can that be?" he wondered. He began following her and almost died of shock when he saw that it was his wife.

"How can this be?" he thought to himself. "I saw the blood on the bed. She could not have survived."

He saw the woman go into the church and he followed her. When he saw her praying, he began to weep bitterly.

After mass, he ran to the priest and told him of the evil deed he had committed. He told how he had stabbed his wife, yet had seen her walking to church that morning.

"How can she be walking around if you killed her?" asked the priest. "I think you had a little too much to drink last night."

The man was insistent and the priest finally decided to go with him to his home. When they got there, they saw the man's wife doing her daily chores as usual.

"Buenos días," said the woman. "Won't you come in, father."

They went into the house. The priest noticed the bloodstains on the floor and realized that the husband had been telling the truth. He asked the wife if she had a prayer that she said before going to sleep each night. The woman said she did and repeated the prayer.

"La Santa Cruz baja del cielo y en mi cuerpo se destienda, La Santa Cruz de mal y peligro. La Santa Cruz me defienda."*

---

*"Holy Cross, come down from heaven and descend on my body, The Holy Cross of evil and danger. Holy Cross, defend me."

After the woman had finished the prayer, the three of them went into the bedroom. They pulled back the covers on the bed and found a bloodstained crucifix. It was scratched and badly bent. When they saw this, they knew they had witnessed a miracle.

The woman forgave her husband and they both lived happily to a ripe old age.

A Stranger Comes to León

MY padrino's* father was a short man who went around Mexico racing horses. He was very good at his profession and was racing his horses in Léon just before the tragedy. On that unfortunate day, he was out of town training and getting his horses in condition for an important race that was coming up.

On the very afternoon that he left, there was a great feast for one of the important men of León who was to marry soon. This man owned several cabarets and had a large share of the business in the town's big night club district.

Imagine! Things had come to such a point in this town that people danced nude at parties and dances, and no one cared anymore about decency.

The feast raged with such force that the revelry, which usually stayed within the bounds of the cabarets,

---

*Godfather's.

spilled out into the sunny city streets. Music could be heard everywhere and great mounds of food covered the tables that had been placed outside.

In the middle of this great spree a stranger, dressed in tattered rags, appeared. Someone in the crowd yelled out a jeering remark and it wasn't long before the whole street resounded with mocking and laughter.

The stranger made his way to the table where the guest of honor was sitting with several of his friends and business partners. The stranger told the rich man that he was on a journey to a distant part of Mexico, had been on the road for several days, and was very weary and hungry.

"Perhaps you can spare me a bit to eat and find me lodging for the night," said the stranger.

But his request was met by a chorus of mocking jeers and laughter. He was told to leave the premises and was escorted to a road on the edge of the city.

The stranger started walking along the dirt road that twisted its way up the valley. He finally came to a hut where an old woman lived. The woman, who was busy spinning wool, was startled by the bearded man who suddenly appeared before her.

"Go into town," he told her. "Tell everybody you meet to leave immediately and start climbing to higher ground." He told her that a great dark cloud in the form of a sandal would form in the sky. "This will be a sign that the time is near," he said.

He also told her to make an honest effort to warn everybody, but that if some of the merrymakers insisted on arguing with her, perhaps thinking her a fool, she should not try to force or beg these people to come.

The old woman set out immediately. When she arrived in León the feast was still going on. She began dashing in and out of the streets of the town. She moved with such nimbleness and shouted with such vigor that many thought her possessed.

The stranger then donned some elegant clothes, climbed into a carriage, and rode back to León. His magnificent carriage shone like gold and the music of his horses' hoofbeats pulled all eyes toward it. Such splendid wood the carriage was made of — it was almost like ivory.

Who was this stranger? Perhaps a French prince on vacation, or maybe an important government official on business.

Everywhere the stranger rode, he was greeted with invitations and compliments. When the rich man saw him ride up, he arose from the chair he was sitting in and went up to greet the stranger, bowing and humbly requesting that he join their table. The elegant stranger was given the place of honor and was waited upon immediately.

Everyone chatted amiably. But when the food was prepared and placed at the stranger's service, he began pouring soup on his vest and smearing food all over his clothes.

The people around him looked on in bewilderment. "What is wrong with him? Has he lost his mind?" they asked each other.

"Sir," asked the rich man, "why are you doing this? You are going to ruin your beautiful clothes."

"I don't deserve to eat this food," the stranger answered. "The ones that really deserve to eat are my clothes and so that is why I am doing this. Earlier in the day I came here as a poor beggar and I was thrown out of town without even a crust of bread."

The stranger then got up and left.

Soon a cloud in the form of a sandal appeared and some of the merrymakers started taking seriously what the old woman had said. Many people started leaving, but others remained behind.

The rich man called for more music and dancing girls in an effort to forget the unpleasant incident. Suddenly, it began raining with such force that it seemed as if water were being poured from a gigantic pail. The water fell in torrents all through the dark night.

In the morning, when my padrino's father was on his way back to León with his horses, he could not find the town. Every road he took led to the edge of the water. In the place where León had been, a large lake had now formed.

This lake is still there today and they say that on Holy days, the church bells ring over the calm waters and the cocks can be heard singing.

Help for a Mule Caravan

A LARGE caravan of muleteers, their beasts laden with merchandise, was journeying to a distant place. They came to a deep canyon with a difficult road. Near a stream, where the ground was soft because of the muddy water, the wagons got stuck.

Despite everything the mule drivers did, they could not get their wagons and teams out of the mud. Some of the drivers were in a state of despair and others cursed savagely, knowing they would have to leave all their merchandise behind to rot or be taken by the Indians. But the leader of the men, instead of despairing or swearing, began praying to the Santo Niño de Atocha.

The muleteers were packing as much merchandise as they could into leather pouches and were preparing to leave. Suddenly, the caravan leader noticed a child walking in the distance and coming towards him. When the child arrived he said to the leader, "Good day, señor, how are you? We don't see strangers in these parts too often."

The muleteer was astonished to see a child in the harsh wilderness. "We have been stuck here for three days and there seems to be no hope that we will get the wagons out of the mud," he said, and they began walking toward the wagons.

In the meantime, the anger of the other mule drivers had reached its peak.

"Muchachos," the leader yelled. "Do me the favor of keeping your mouths shut. Can't you see there is a child here?"

"What's the difference?" grumbled the muleteers.

"I tell you to shut up," the man shouted back, and they finally quieted down.

By that time the mud had reached the top of the wagon wheels. The little boy asked the men to detach a group of mules that had been put together in an effort to free one of the wagons.

"Put one mule to every wagon as usual," the boy said. "Then get into your wagons, everyone."

The child took the reins and cracked the whip. Under the eyes of the bewildered muleteers, the wagons began slowly pulling out, one by one. Soon every wagon was out of the mud and on the road again.

After they had traveled awhile, the man asked the child where he lived so that he could take him home. The child told the man to leave him there on the road.

"I'll find my way home," he said.

The man then asked the child what he wanted.

"You can have anything you want — just ask for it," he told the child.

The child answered that he wanted a little dress for Santa María de Atocha.

When the man turned to look, the child was gone. Then he knew who the miraculous child had been. He sent the muleteers on ahead, and he himself went to Plateros to give the dress to the Virgin and his grateful thanks to the Santo Niño.

The Cripple and
Señor San Antonio

THERE was a young man who lived a very sad and unhappy life. He had been born a cripple and had spent all his life on crutches.

For years and years he had prayed to Señor San Antonio for good health. He wanted to experience life like normal young men his age. He wanted to dance with pretty señoritas and ride on spirited horses. He continued to pray, day after day, hoping that Señor San Antonio might hear his plea.

The years went by quickly and his youth began to fade. He began to doubt that he would ever be healed. More time went by and his doubt gave way to despair and finally to anger.

"What did I waste my time for?" he raged. "Señor San Antonio is going to pay dearly."

One day he asked his cousin, who owned a carriage, if he would take him to the temple of Señor San Antonio. His cousin, who was a deeply religious man and had made the pilgrimage before, readily agreed.

Everything was finally in order and they set out on the road to Puebla. They traveled the rest of the day with nothing unusual happening. The crippled man concealed his anger behind some shallow conversation. His cousin could not have imagined in his wildest dreams what the young man's intentions were.

Before the cousins knew it, the first stars had begun to appear. They rode on until they came to a clearing where they decided to camp overnight. The place was swarming with muleteers in transit to distant parts of Mexico.

The cousins made their campsite next to a group from Jalisco and prepared their evening meal. After they had eaten, they took out cigarettes to have a smoke before retiring. One of the mule drivers, sitting by the campfire next to theirs, was telling a story and they lay down to listen.

He was telling of a boy that he was putting through college. He said that many years before, the boy's father had been his compadre. He told how his compadre had tried to kill him in order to steal his silver pieces. He described the way in which the bandit had met his tragic end, with a bullet lodged in his forehead.

The tale of the unfortunate bandit proved to the crippled man more than ever that it didn't pay to trust anyone. He got into his blankets and went to sleep, angrier than ever with Señor San Antonio.

The next morning the cousins were on their way again. They were in a mountainous area and the traveling was very rough. As they came around a bend, they noticed a man walking ahead of them on the road. They offered him a ride and he accepted. After traveling for awhile, the stranger began telling an amazing tale. The cousins were soon spellbound and listened attentively.

"A contract between my father and the devil was signed in blood before I was born," he told them. "I didn't find out that my soul was promised to the devil until after I had become a priest." He said that after much difficulty, he had finally obtained the contract. "A bandit, who was the devil's compadre, introduced me to the devil. When I came back from hell, the bandit was so awed by what I had seen there that he repented. He confessed to me all about the evil life he had been leading and then died in my arms."

The little wagon carrying the three men rolled on down the road. The crippled man listened to what the priest said and began to have second thoughts about his own situation. "What appears certain is not always so," he concluded. He began to wonder if he should not give Señor San Antonio more time.

When the little wagon came to a crossroads, the priest got off and the two cousins continued on their way alone. They had been on the road for a long time and were nearing their destination. The crippled man's mind was now aflame. The influence of the priest had been profound and he began to have second thoughts once again about what he was planning to do. But his bitterness was so strong that it still overpowered him.

Finally, the cousins arrived at the temple. The crippled man was helped by his cousin all the way to the altar. At last he was face to face with Señor San Antonio.

"Enough of all this," he said. "I begged you and begged you but you never answered my prayers. You're good for nothing."

The crippled man reached into his pocket, took out a rock, cocked his arm, and threw the rock with all his might. But when he looked up, he saw that Señor San Antonio had caught the rock in his hand and was about to throw it back at him. The crippled man was so startled, he ran out of the church as fast as a jackrabbit.

When he got outside, he suddenly realized that his own legs had carried him out. He began weeping and asking Señor San Antonio to forgive him for his lack of faith.

The Old Woman
And El Señor

THERE was once an elderly señora who spun wool on her spinning wheel as she daydreamed her old age away. Day after day in her white room she would think, "How beautiful my room is, but how I wish I had a statue of the Señor."

The señora's house was situated on a rural rancho and, for this reason, she prayed all the harder that a traveling merchant would happen along and sell her a statue of the Señor, before death asked for her.

One day, the señora's nephews and nieces were playing in the yard when a man appeared. "Where is the lady of the house?" he wanted to know. "Ask her if she will buy a statue of the Señor from me."

The children ran up to where the old woman was spinning. "Mama, mama," they cried. "There's a man out there who says he'll sell you a Señor."

73

The señora dropped what she was doing and ran outside to greet the stranger.

"Won't you buy the Señor?" asked the man.

"Oh, kind sir, how did you know that I so desired a statue of the Señor?" asked the old woman. "Let me go and get you some money."

The señora started inside but the stranger stopped her. "Here, take the Señor in with you. Then you can bring me out the money," he said.

The señora went inside the house, but when she came out with the money, the merchant had disappeared. She asked her nieces and nephews to help her find the man. She even paid gritones* who shouted her message from every corner of the rancho. But her efforts to locate the merchant were in vain. He had disappeared as suddenly as he had appeared.

The days passed, then turned into months, and the incident with the merchant was forgotten. The señora had a little altar built in the corner of her room and there she placed the Señor.

One day, as she dozed at her spinning wheel, the Señor caught fire from one of the candles on top of the altar. By the time the old woman awoke, the Señor was badly burned and she began to weep bitterly. She picked him up, took him to the river, and washed his wounds with cotton in the cool stream. Then she sent him off to Guadalajara to be repaired. But as soon as he got back to the señora's house, all the paint and plaster fell off,

---

*Criers.

74

and the wounds from the fire revealed themselves again.

The Señor was sent away to be repaired two more times. However, as soon as he was returned to his altar, his wounds became visible again.

The years went by and the story of the Señor spread far and wide. One could hear accounts of the Señor even in the most remote corners of the haciendas. "Even if it did not rain today, why worry," people would say. "We have faith in the Señor and we can always go to him."

When the old señora died, she left money for a small temple where the Señor could wait for those who came with problems or to pay him honor. People from the different regions would come searching for the Señor, arriving in processions and dancing with their pointed lances and headdresses swaying in the wind. From as far away as a hundred miles they came.

It so happened that during a serious drought, when it had not rained in long months and the dry spell continued even after the Señor had been thrice marched around in procession, the people became highly upset and emotional. It was precisely in this state of mind that a local rich man uttered the blasphemous words, "So your Señor can make it rain, eh? Well, if he does, I will swallow every last drop of water through my ass."

He was sorry he had said these words because a terrible thunderstorm was soon overhead, pouring down buckets of rain and swelling the sun-parched arroyos. It rained day and night, day after day.

The rich ranchero's house and barn lay in a large clearing where two arroyos crossed. After the third day of rain, his property resembled a swamp. The storm raged with such strength that even his mesquite trees were uprooted, and the arroyos that crossed his property were turned into mighty rivers. Pigs, cows, horses, chickens — everything the man owned was being washed away, even the wheat that had been stored in his barn.

The ranchero was desperate and he got on his horse and somehow made it to Santa María. There was not a soul to be seen anywhere. He went to the church and found everyone inside. "Forgive me," he said rushing to the altar. He got on his knees and begged to be forgiven. Everyone prayed.

When it first began to rain, the people were very happy. However, it had now rained for over nine weeks and they were asking the Señor to stop the rain. Every once in awhile a woman would even scatter a pinch of salt in the form of a cross. They were all happy to see the ranchero arrive and recant his words.

Later that same day, the first signs appeared that the weather was going to calm down. It continued raining throughout the night, only now it seemed like a drizzle compared to before. The people slept peacefully.

On the following morning, the sunshine finally broke through. The people began the big job of cleaning up all the mess, but went about their business happily.

The ranchero returned to his home. He had learned a good lesson and never did he again doubt El Señor de la Santa Escuelita.

The Santo Niño
Saves a Friendship

THERE were two young rancheros who loved each other dearly and were inseparable. The sun sparkled against the leaves on the nopales as they chatted aimlessly on the road to the fair. On and on they walked, without a care, enjoying the beautiful afternoon. They could hardly wait to get to the fair. There was going to be music, tequila, and plenty of young señoritas.

Quite unintentionally, their conversation turned toward the question of money. "I have fifty pesos," said Pablo. "With that amount of money, I can enjoy myself better than any prince." Pedro made no response. He had only thirty pesos.

The farther they walked, the more Pedro thought about the difference. Jealousy was beginning to take control of him and instead of enjoying the birds' happy

77

songs, he became more and more bitter. Pablo noticed that his friend had grown quiet but thought he was simply tired.

It was getting late and the friends began to look for a good campsite. They found a clearing, built a fire under the twinkling stars, and had their dinner.

Pablo was the first to retire. His dreams were happy and tranquil and the thought of death was as far away as the twinkling stars above his head.

Pedro's mind, on the contrary, was now filled with dark thoughts. He had decided to kill his best friend.

While Pablo slept peacefully, Pedro quietly went away from the campsite and found a large rock. He took it back to where his friend was sleeping and dropped it on his head. So great was the force of the blow that the rock broke in two and Pablo's brains were smeared all over the ground. Pedro then reached into his friend's vest pocket, took the fifty pesos, and went on his way.

When he had traveled a long way and was approaching the fair, Pedro began thinking. "What have I done? Santo Niño de Atocha, don't permit my friend to be dead."

He began to weep bitterly as the weight of his evil deed crushed down upon him. He started running back with the agonizing strength of desperation. The people on their way to the fair, in a gay and festive mood, could only stare in bewilderment. On and on he ran with such fervor that, as he was getting close to the place where he had committed the murder, he was stumbling, falling and even dragging himself.

When he reached the exact spot, the corpse of the dead ranchero slowly began to rise, the rock still embedded in his skull.

"Santo Niño de Atocha," Pedro cried wildly. He put his arms around his friend and wept uncontrollably.

They began to walk down the road and didn't stop until they came to Plateros and the Santo Niño's temple. Pedro, still weeping, took the rock out of his friend's head and placed it at the feet of the Santo Niño. When he looked up, he noticed that Pablo's wound had healed.

Pedro's joy was immense, but he still felt remorse in his heart and fell down at his friend's feet begging forgiveness. Pablo reached down and pulled his friend up and they both walked along toward the fair, as happy as could be.

The Santo Niño
Visits a Prison

THERE was once a woman, condemned to life imprisonment, in the federal prison at Quiroga. In a jealous rage over the affections of a lover, she had stabbed her rival through the heart.

Her life was lived a million times over during the long days inside her lonely cell. Every evening she would see herself in a new vision, sometimes as a little girl running along the dusty streets with the dog she loved so well, sometimes as a young señorita discovering the unscrupulous lust of the brothel. But her victim's insane scream always shattered even her most profound dreams.

Then she would pray, as only a person in such a situation can pray. And she would commend herself to the Santo Niño and ask him to bear some of the weight of her regrets and sorrow.

The years went by in this manner and the poor woman's health started to fade, just as her dreams had. Now she would leave the meager ration of food, that had once been her sustenance, on the tin plate that the guard carried back to the kitchens.

One day, as she stood staring at the bars of her cell, she noticed a little boy in the corner. She was very startled and thought she was imagining the whole thing.

"How did you get in here?" she asked him.

The visitor told her that he had slipped in when one of the guards opened the door. He then pulled out some food from his basket and asked her to eat something. She did not want to eat at first, but talking to someone after all those years strengthened her spirit and gave her an appetite. After she had finished eating, she looked up to say something to the child. But he was no longer in the cell.

The rest of the day she could only think of the little boy and what had occurred. When she finally fell asleep late that night, she had a dream. She was a basket weaved in light and with a bleeding heart inside.

When she awoke from her deep sleep she rubbed her eyes, looked up, and noticed the little boy once again. He took some food out of his basket and offered it to her. When she had finished eating, he told her that he must be on his way but that he would return one last time and then she was to go away with him. Before the woman could question the boy, he had vanished.

"He did say I was to go away with him," she said to herself. "But how can I get out of here with all the steel bars and guards everywhere?" This thought occupied her mind the whole day as she paced back and forth in her cell.

When night came, she lay down on the floor and was starting to doze off to sleep when she noticed something in the corner of the room. The child glowed like a fire.

She heard his voice telling her to follow and not to look at anything but him. He told her that as soon as they were outside, she would see a star in the sky and that she was to follow it.

She saw the little boy going through the steel bars and thick brick walls, and she followed him until they were outside. She then began following the star and continued walking all night without once taking her eyes off of it, exactly as she had been told.

Who knows what might have happened to her if she had looked down. Perhaps she would have fallen down. Or maybe she would have stayed there in the unimaginable void.

When dawn appeared, the woman lost sight of the star and finally began looking around. There were people all around her. The marketplace was in a frantic state as the peasants brought their provisions before the market opened. The town chattered with early morning activities. It was as if the woman was in a dream.

She walked down the street until she came to a restaurant where she asked for a cup of coffee.

"Can you tell me the name of this town?" she asked the people there.

"Why, this is Plateros," they answered in bewilderment.

She began telling them how she had followed the star and walked all night.

"I left Quiroga at nightfall yesterday," she said.

All the people standing around began thinking that perhaps she was a madwoman. "How could she have possibly crossed all those states in one night?" they cried.

The woman then asked the people if they could tell her where the church of the Santo Niño was. But before they had a chance to answer, church bells began ringing nearby and the woman fell to her knees.

THE FOIBLES

OF MAN AND BEAST

The pichilingis were a nuisance to everyone, but sometimes they would choose a particular family to annoy. My great-grandmother used to tell this story.

There was a family that had somehow attracted the attention of the pichilingis. Every single member of the family was a victim of their pranks. They would be sitting down for a meal with the food on the table ready to eat when suddenly a chunk of mule droppings would fly through the air and land in the beans. Or they would go out to milk the cows in the morning and all they would find was a puddle of milk on the ground. The pichilingis had been at it again.

Needless to say, the family soon reached the point of despair.

"What are we to do?" the wife asked her husband. "Everything is always disappearing. Why, we can't even eat peacefully anymore."

She wanted to leave at once, but her husband was reluctant.

"How can we forsake our house and abandon all our friends?" he wanted to know. "After all, I was born on this ranch."

But the husband, who was also tired of the pichilingis' pranks, finally agreed to leave.

The family packed its belongings and placed them on the burros. Everyone in the community came to see them off. They all knew why the family was leaving.

After a sad farewell, the family started down the road. They traveled all afternoon until it began to get dark. "There's a clearing just ahead," said the husband. "We'll camp there tonight."

In the distance they could see the lights from the campfires. When they finally arrived at the campsite, they unpacked and prepared their dinner. The wife's spirits were high and she prepared a wonderful meal. When they had finished eating it, the husband asked her to make some coffee.

"Dios mío!" cried the wife. "I have forgotten the coffeepot."

"It's over here," they heard someone shout.

They turned toward a large mesquite where the voice had come from. To their great surprise, they saw a dozen or so pichilingis sitting around a campfire. The silhouette of the coffeepot flashed with the movement of the fire. All the unfortunate people could do was shake their heads in disbelief and go to sleep.

When they awoke the next morning, they found the coffee pot in the middle of their campfire.

"What's the use of going on?" said the husband. "If the pichilingis are going to be with us, we might as well be at home."

The family packed the burros and started back home.

The pichilingis stayed with the people who lived on the ranchos for many years. But one day, they suddenly went away and never came back.

They went to a mountain called the "Casa Santa.*"

_____

*Holy House.

89

That's where Noah's Ark is sitting. The pichilingis are the ones that take care of the ark.

They say that a lot of people go to the mountain to visit. You can go inside, but if you have evil thoughts or if you steal something, the pichilingis won't let you out again.

The Reason for Turtles

THERE was an old lady who was very poor and she would go to her daughter's house for meals in order to supplement her meager diet. But her daughter wasn't always happy to see her when she arrived.

"Here comes my mother again," the daughter would say to herself. "And when we barely have enough to eat ourselves."

One day the daughter was busy preparing dinner for her husband, who was still at work. She had gone to the market earlier that day and, while browsing around, had come across the plumpest chicken she had ever seen.

"How much do you want for it?" she had asked the vendor.

"I'm asking twenty-five centavos."

The daughter had only eighteen centavos but after a bit of bargaining, the vendor had finally agreed to sell the fowl to her.

Just then the daughter heard the sound of her mother's footsteps.

"Of all days, why did she have to come today?" she thought aloud. "The day that I prepare my plump chicken."

"Buenas tardes, daughter," the old lady called out.

The daughter didn't answer but, quick as a wink, put a pot on top of the savory hen sitting on the table. "I hope my mother doesn't stay very long today," she thought to herself.

"How have you been, daughter?" asked the old lady.

"Just fine," the daughter replied curtly and continued with her household chores.

The old lady was aware that her daughter was ignoring her but she kept trying to start a conversation anyway.

The afternoon was going by quickly. It would soon be time for the husband to come home from work. "When is she going to leave?" the daughter asked herself. She was now desperate and kept dropping little hints, trying to get rid of her mother.

"Mama, it's very late now," she said. "Don't you think it's time you should be going home?"

The old lady sat there for a few minutes and then finally left for home.

When her mother had gone, the daughter sat down to wait for her husband. She then noticed that a swarm of flies had come into the kitchen after her mother had departed. She took a large tablecloth and spread it over the table to keep the flies away from the food.

When her husband came home, he went to draw some water from the well. While he was washing, his wife sat down at the table.

"Won't my husband be happy when he sees the chicken?" she thought. "We'll be able to eat to our heart's delight."

The husband came into the house and sat down at the table. "And what have you prepared for dinner this evening?" he asked.

"I have a little surprise for you," his wife beamed.

But when she pulled the tablecloth back, a turtle started walking across the table.

"What is that?" the man asked.

The startled woman told him that she didn't know. "I had prepared a chicken that I bought this morning," she told him.

In the meantime, the turtle jumped on the floor and left the house.

The husband and wife became very frightened and went to summon the priest.

"What has happened?" the priest asked as soon as he saw them.

They told him about the strange incident that had occurred.

"Why did this happen to you?" asked the priest. "Have you been leading a good life?"

The woman then remembered how she had thrown her mother out of the house. "I have done a very bad thing," she cried. "I didn't want to share the chicken with my mother, so I forced her out of the house."

When the husband heard this he was furious. "If you throw your own mother out of the house, how will you treat my relatives?" He called her an evil woman and showered her with a stream of obscenities.

Finally, the priest intervened. "It was a curse from God," he said. He told the couple that respecting and loving one's parents was the most important thing in life.

From that day on, the wife's attitude toward her mother changed completely. She would often invite her over and would sit and visit with her for hours. And so it remained until the old woman's death.

That is why we have turtles today. If you break the beak of a chicken, it will look like a turtle. The feet of the turtle look like the wings of a chicken without feathers.

They say, anyway, that this is why we have turtles. If you think about it, it seems right — maybe it is.

My Godmother's Story
Of Buried Treasure

EVERYWHERE you went, the bells would be ringing and the people would be in a festive spirit. Holy Week ensured joyous feelings.

The women made fritters that were to be eaten with hot atolito. Children played in the dusty streets. And the man drank their pulque.

In the evenings all the people of the rancho would gather together. Lanterns would be brought out and the people would play games.

Some drew squares on the ground and played "bebeleche." To play, someone would throw a rock on one of the squares and then hop along on one leg. He had to step in every square except where the rock had fallen.

Others would clasp hands in a large circle to play "the nun and the devils." The girl who happened to be in the middle of the circle was called the nun, and someone outside became the devil. When the circle opened, the girl would run as fast as she could because the devil would be right on her skirts. She would then try to run back to the safety of the circle. They say that one night my tío Casimiro caught the nun and carried her all the way to the river.

Toward midnight, the people who were still awake would climb on the roofs of their houses. From there they could look for the fires that revealed where buried treasure was hidden.

There was a large group where we lived — Simonito, Casimiro, and my tía Chana were there. The women would all pray while the men and children scanned the darkness for signs of a fire.

Suddenly one night, one of the children let out a yell. "Over there! Can you see it over there?"

The fire was about a mile away and came from the direction of Julian Aguilar's ranch.

When the people in the group went to investigate the next morning, they found that the place where the fire had been was indeed inside Señor Aguilar's property. His ranch was fenced in and the people were wondering what to do. "If we find the treasure, perhaps they will give us something," someone suggested. They finally decided to go and ask for permission to search.

When they arrived at Don Julian Aguilar's house, they found his wife sitting on the front porch.

Doña María Palos was an enormous woman. She was so heavy that a burro was unable to carry her. When she went to San Juan, she had to be hauled on a mule. The people told her what they had seen and asked if she would give them permission to dig on her property.

"Of course, go right ahead and dig," she said.

When the people heard this, they were overjoyed. Simonito went and got a pick and one of the other men got a shovel.

Five hours later they had dug so far into the ground that Simonito's head barely reached the top of the hole. During this time the women had not ceased praying for help to find the treasure. But, none had been found and the men were growing very tired. A few of the people in the party had even gone home.

Suddenly there was a loud clang and everyone froze. Simonito had hit something made of metal with his pick. Two of the men crawled into the hole and started digging the dirt away with their hands.

Casimiro, one of the men inside the hole, finally yelled out, "It's the ear of a casket."

Everyone was overjoyed. The women, now almost in a trance, continued praying fervently. "I wonder how much she will give us," cried Simonito. The men kept digging and soon the whole side of the brass casket could be seen.

At the first sound of clanking metal, one of the children ran as fast as his legs would carry him to Don Julian Aguilar's home.

"We've found the treasure," he shouted excitedly.

María Palos and her maid were preparing dinner in the kitchen. As soon as she heard what the young boy was saying, she lumbered out of the house. The servants helped her get on the mule and off she went to where the people were digging.

When she arrived, my tía Chana ran up to her. "Señora, blessed be God!" she cried. María Palos pushed her roughly out of the way.

"Stop digging," she yelled. "Julian buried that money there."

The men stopped digging and the people grew very quiet. What had been joyous expectation, a few moments before, was suddenly turned into sad disbelief.

María Palos told them her husband had buried the treasure years ago. She then told them that they had better leave because Don Aguilar would soon be home and would be furious if he saw what they were up to.

While Doña María was still talking, the sound of gurgling water was heard. Everyone looked in the hole where the brass casket had been. Simonito even jumped into the hole, now half filled with water, and started feeling around with his shovel.

"I can't feel the casket anymore," he told them.

He groped some more, still trying to locate the casket. Finally, after several more efforts, he gave up and climbed out of the hole.

That evening my people went to bed no richer than the night before. However, they had learned a great lesson. The woman's greed had been stronger than the people's good will. The money didn't go to God, nor did it go to the devil.

Three Challenges
For King Solomon

ONE day King Solomon, who had grown very old, called his son to him.

"Son, listen carefully," he said. "I am growing old, but I have discovered a way to be reborn. I want you to kill me and chop me in little pieces. Put all the pieces inside a burlap sack and secure it very tightly. Then go and dig a hole six feet deep, spread steer manure in it, drop in the sack, and seal the hole up again."

The surprised son could only listen.

"No air must get into the hole until it is time for you to take me out," King Solomon continued. He also told his son that no one but he and his wife were to know where he was buried or attend him after rebirth.

The son was awed and dismayed but agreed to carry out his father's wishes.

News of King Solomon's disappearance spread to the far kingdoms of the world. Everyone wanted to know what had become of him. Many were deeply saddened and concerned by his disappearance. Others, mainly the high ranking nobles of his court, started to scheme and plot to take over his throne. But, not knowing King Solomon's fate, they hesitated to make a move.

When it was almost time for the king to be reborn, the leaders of his court began to get restless. They summoned his son and questioned him about his father. The son persisted in answering that he did not know a thing.

"Only heaven knows where my father is," he kept saying.

But the nobles of the court, who were very cunning, insisted that he did know something and finally decided that he should be tried by a court of law. The High Priest proclaimed that, if he could perform three tasks given to him by the court, he would be able to prove his innocence.

The day of the trial finally arrived and the king's son appeared before the judges. "Your first task is this," they told him. "When you appear before us tomorrow, you will be shod but yet unshod."

The young man started back home in dismay. "How can I return shod and yet unshod?" he wondered. Finally, after much thinking, he went to the place where King Solomon was buried.

100

"Father, father," he lamented. "All is lost for both of us. The judges have asked me to return tomorrow, shod but yet unshod."

King Solomon answered from his grave. "Son, cut the soles out of your shoes and wear only the tops. This way you will be shod and yet unshod."

The following day the judges were waiting for King Solomon's son. When he appeared in front of them, they looked at each other in disbelief. He had been able to meet their challenge. They then told the son to come back the next day, mounted but yet on foot.

Once again the son was unable to solve the riddle. And again he decided to go and consult his father.

"What do they want you to do this time, son?" asked King Solomon.

"Father," the son answered, "tomorrow they want me to return mounted and yet on foot. What shall I do?"

And King Solomon told him, "Before going in, find a large goat, saddle it, and ride into the court dragging your feet. This way you will arrive mounted but on foot."

When the young man arrived before the judges, they were all amazed. He had again been able to meet their challenge. But still they did not give up. They told King Solomon's son to leave once more and return the next day with a friend and an enemy.

As soon as the son left the palace, he rushed to the place where his father was buried. He was extremely happy because this was the last task he would have to accomplish.

"Father, this time they want me to bring a friend and an enemy," he said.

When King Solomon heard this he became very sad and said, "It was not willed that I be reborn."

He then told his son, "When you go tomorrow, take your wife and dog with you. When you arrive at the palace gate, tell your wife to wait there and take the dog inside with you. When you go up before the judges, start kicking your dog as hard as you can, then send him a short distance away. When you call him and he comes back to you, they will see that your friend is there. Then go back to the gate and shove your wife inside. This will be your enemy."

The son was puzzled at his father's words. "How can my wife be my enemy?" he asked.

King Solomon told his son that he would get his answer the following day.

When King Solomon's son appeared in front of the judges, he had his dog with him as his father had instructed. He began beating the dog, then chased him away. When the dog had gone a little distance, he called, "Come here," and the dog came right back, wagging his tail.

The son then went back to the gate where his wife was waiting. "Let's go," he yelled and began pushing and shoving her inside.

The embarrassed woman became furious. "This is the way you thank me for all the help I gave you and your father!" she raged. And in a few seconds she had revealed everything about her husband's secret.

That evening, the men from the court went to uncover the king. When they dug him out he was already formed, but they had exposed him to the air too soon and he could not be reborn.

This is the reason why, to this day, nobody has ever been able to discover the whereabouts of Solomon's grave.

The Farmer Who Listened To His Livestock

THERE was once a ranchero who lived with his wife on a large hacienda. As a young man, he had rescued a pichilingi that had fallen into the river and was drowning. As a reward for this deed, the pichilingi had given him the ability to understand the speech of animals. The pichilingi had warned him, however, that the moment he revealed the secret to anyone else, he would lose his magical ability.

Thus, one of the ranchero's greatest pleasures was to go around the hacienda and listen to the different animals talking. One day, he noticed an ox coming back from the fields, looking tired and dejected. He also noticed a burro jumping friskily around the ox, just as happy as could be. The ranchero didn't say a word but decided that from then on, he would listen to the conversation between the ox and the burro.

One day, when the ox had returned from the fields, the burro went up to him and started a conversation.

"What's new?" he asked the ox.

"I'm dead tired and I need some rest," answered the ox.

"Why are you so tired?" again asked the burro. "All you ever do is walk back and forth all day."

"It may appear so," lamented the ox, "but when I come home from work, I am so tired that I cannot even eat."

The ranchero, who had overheard the conversation, became very interested. "I'm sure going to keep my eye on these two," he chuckled to himself.

The next day the burro came strutting into the stable. He was very spirited and appeared to be the happiest burro in the world. When the ox saw him, he was filled with admiration.

"I wish I was as happy as you are," he said.

"You're a fool," replied the burro. "If I had a pair of horns like yours, you would never see me out in the field."

The ox shook his horns. "How can my horns make my life any easier?" he asked.

"Don't be so stupid," the burro said. "In the morning, when the labrador comes to harness you, get up and pretend that you are very angry. Kick up the dust with your hoofs and point your horns at him."

It didn't take long for the burro to convince the ox. "What a fool I have been," the ox thought.

When the labrador entered the stable the following

morning, he received the surprise of his life. In place of the docile ox, he found a ferocious beast kicking up dust and glaring menacingly at him. Every time the labrador attempted to put his harness on, the ox would charge the man and send him scurrying out of the stable. The labrador finally gave up and ran to report the news to his master.

"Ay, Amo," he said. "I don't know what's come over the ox, but he's in a very bad temper and won't let me get near him. Every time I try to get his harness on, he begins kicking up dust and intimidating me with his horns."

The ranchero started laughing. "If the ox is still in a bad mood tomorrow, you take the burro in his place," he told the labrador.

"But sir," the man protested. "What can a burro do in the fields?"

"It doesn't matter," replied his master. "Take him anyway."

The next morning the ox pretended to be angry again. The burro, who had been sleeping peacefully, was harnessed, and was forced to labor all day in the fields.

When the burro arrived back that evening, he was barely able to walk. Nevertheless, as soon as he noticed the ox, he began to roll himself in the dirt. He seemed as happy as could be.

The ox was very surprised to see him like this. "How can you be so happy?" he asked. "Didn't they work you hard today?"

The burro thought for a moment, then answered. "I can't understand why you made such a fuss. I don't find it hard at all."

The ranchero, who was listening to the conversation, had to use all of his willpower to keep from laughing. He knew that the burro was trying to trick the ox into going back to work.

The ox quickly adjusted to his new role. When the labrador came to harness him the next day, he put on his act again. Every time the poor man tried to put the harness on, the ox would send him scurrying. After several attempts, the man finally gave up and went to look for the burro.

When the burro arrived home that evening, he pretended that he was still in high spirits and began rolling in the dirt again. "What a fool I've been," he said. "If I had started working the fields before, I would now have the strength of ten mules." Then he changed to another topic. "You can't imagine what I heard today," he said. "A terrible rumor concerning you has spread all over the hacienda."

The curious ox wanted to know more about the rumor, but the burro refused to answer and went off to bed.

The next day events repeated themselves in exactly the same way.

By the time the burro arrived home from the fields this time, the ox was dying of curiosity. "Tell me what is being said," he pleaded. After much persuasion, the burro finally agreed.

"I didn't want to tell you because, in truth, it makes me very sad," he began. "I overheard the master saying that you have become a useless burden. He's planning to send you to the butcher."

The ox became very scared and began bellowing. "I don't want to die," he cried. "What shall I do, dear friend, what shall I do?"

The burro pretended to be in deep contemplation, but after a few moments he began to speak. "The master thinks you're a freeloader and a good-for-nothing. He knows you haven't been going to work all week. Now if you want to save your hide, you'd better do exactly as I tell you. In the morning, when the labrador comes into the stable, don't wait. Go up to him and start licking the harness. In this way, he'll know that you want to go back to work."

The labrador came into the stable early the next morning. By now he was very frightened of the ox and the only reason he still tried to harness him was that his master insisted on it. Therefore, he was astounded when he noticed the ox licking the harness, and even more so when he heard loud laughter coming from outside.

The master had just happened to be passing by and had heard what was going on. His wife, who was watering the plants outside the house, heard his laughter.

"Why are you laughing?" she asked.

"For no reason at all, woman," he answered. "Simply out of happiness."

The woman insisted on knowing and became very angry when he wouldn't tell her.

A week passed by, with the woman continuously nagging her husband. And then another week. It went on so long that finally the man was willing to tell his wife just to get some peace.

The master's dog, who was unable to stand any more arguments, scurried out to the courtyard. As he turned the corner, he ran into the cock and all his hens.

Kee kee dee kee! Kee kee dee kee! The cock walked about fluttering his wings and proudly displaying his tail. Suddenly, the dog leaped on him and started chasing him all over the courtyard.

The cock flew on top of a fence post. "What's wrong with you?" he protested. "Why are you trying to bite me? Aren't we from the same house, the same family?"

"I'm sorry," replied the dog, "but what I just heard put me in such a rage that I couldn't stand seeing you so happy and carefree. The master is going to tell his secret to his wife."

The cock waited until the dog had calmed down. "The master shouldn't be a fool," he said. "Look at me — all these hens but I'm still the king. The master should take a lesson." The cock hopped down from the fence post and sent the hens flying with shoves and slaps from his wings.

Meanwhile, the ranchero was listening attentively from the door.

"What the master should do is go to the river, gather some quince branches, and break them on his wife's seat until she stops asking questions," said the emboldened cock.

Upon hearing this, the ranchero got his determination back. He walked to the river, found the branches, and hurried back to his house. His wife looked at the sticks.

"Do you still want to know why I laughed?" he asked her.

"I sure do," she replied and began nagging again.

Pas, pas — the ranchero whacked her a few times.

Soon the woman yelled, "No! No! I don't want to know anymore."

When the dog heard this, he rushed out of the house to tell the other animals. "We won, we won," he shouted.

Needless to say, there was much rejoicing at the hacienda that day.

The Poor Rich Man's Son Gets a Second Chance

THERE was a rich man who lived with his only son. His wife had died shortly after the baby's birth, and he had never remarried. But, although he loved his son dearly, he was never able to get close to him.

The years went by quickly and before long, the son was a grown man. However, the father soon realized that his beloved son had taken a wrong path in life. He was too extravagant with his money, and there was always a group of merrymakers following him wherever he went. It was not uncommon for him to spend as much as two or three hundred pesos a night, drinking and playing cards at one of the local cabarets.

The rich man, whose health was failing, realized that he did not have long to live. He tried several times to direct his son to a better life, but all his good advice seemed to go in one ear and come right out the other.

More time passed and the rich man, who was now very old, was on his deathbed. He asked one of his servants to go and fetch his son.

The servant looked all over town and finally found the boy in a dingy cantina. The son was so drunk that he was hardly able to walk home. When he finally arrived at his father's bedside, his father asked the priest and servants gathered around to wait outside.

Once alone with his son, the father said, "I won't ask you to change your ways, Carlos; I've already tried for too many years. However, I want you to make me one last promise. If the day ever comes when you find yourself tired of life and desperate with need, I want you to take this rope, throw it around the beam of the main room, and hang yourself.

The young man agreed to the strange request, and the old man gave him his blessing and died peacefully.

In his will, the father left his entire estate to his son. The young man soon forgot his promise and went back to his life of sin. More than ever now, the festive crowd gathered around him.

Little by little the rancho, that his father had managed so carefully, began to deteriorate. The servants, who had loyally served his father, left one by one as they were never paid on time and their families often had to go hungry. Soon the ranch was in a state of complete decay and only a handful of the most faithful servants were left.

For the village's saint day, a great celebration had been planned. There was to be horse racing, cock fights and many other festivities. When the day finally arrived, the young man went to the bank to draw out some money. To his great surprise, he was told that there wasn't a single peso left. This threw him into a state of shock but he could only lament and wonder where all the money had gone.

He left the bank and went to the celebration. When he got there, everyone was in a festive mood. His friends, who were used to his extravagance, greeted him warmly. "Where have you been, Carlos? We've been waiting for you." But when they found out that the young man's money had run out, they promptly made up excuses and left.

The young man started to walk around in a daze. All around him the people were enjoying themselves, but he didn't even have enough money to buy himself a drink. "Where are all my friends now?" he wondered. He started walking home and as he turned a corner, he met the son of one of his servants.

"What is the matter, Carlos?" asked the servant, startled by the dejected look on his master's face.

Carlos told him the sad story and started to cry. When the servant's son heard the story, he invited Carlos to have a drink and treated him for the rest of the afternoon. By evening, both young men were very drunk. Carlos finally thanked his servant and started on his way.

"What a fool I have been," he lamented. "I have

thrown away everything my father lived for, and I threw it away on hypocrites and false friends." As he walked toward his home, he remembered the promise he had made to his father many years before.

When he arrived at the house, he found the rope and looped it around the beam as his father had instructed. "So this is how it will all end," he sighed. He said a prayer, kicked the stool out from under his feet, and felt the rope tighten around his neck. . . . He hung for an instant, then the wooden beam gave way and came crashing down. The poor devil was sent sprawling.

As Carlos lay on the floor, a small golden trickle started dropping from a hole in the ceiling. This small trickle became a torrent, and soon the bewildered son was lying half-buried in gold coins.

After a night of deep thought, the young man called his servants to an early meeting. Much to everyone's surprise, he announced that the servant's son, who had befriended him, was to become his partner.

From that day on, things began to change. Carlos gave up his life of rowdiness and became the hardest worker who had ever lived.

When his old friends heard about his renewed wealth, they came rushing back. But instead of the warm reception they expected, Carlos told them not to ever appear again unless they wanted to get a taste of his bullwhip. Soon the rancho was blooming with prosperity. Carlos, for the first time in his life, felt at peace.

And forever after, Carlos held a blessing in his heart for his father's generosity and wisdom.

A Reward for Honesty

THERE was a man who was very poor, and tired of being so poor. One day he said to his wife, "I'm going to look around. Maybe I can find some work." The wife was glad that her husband was making an effort to better their wretched existence. She packed a lunch for him and off he went down the road.

When he had been walking for a couple of hours an old beggar woman, squatting under the shade of a large cactus, managed to catch his eye. But he ignored her and continued down the road. He had walked only ten paces, however, when he suddenly changed his mind and started back to where the old woman was squatting.

"I don't have much to give you," he said to her. "But you can have one of the tacos from my lunch."

The old beggar thanked him heartily and he continued on his way.

Farther down the road he met another woman who was begging. The man looked into his lunch bag and noticed that there were two tacos left. He felt very sorry for the old lady and decided to give her one of the tacos.

"Oh, well," he thought. "I still have one taco left for myself."

When he had gone still farther down the road, he noticed a man lying by the side of a creek. When he got closer, he noticed that the stranger had a broken leg.

"I've been without food for three days," lamented the stranger.

The man gave the stranger his last taco and went to find some branches to make a splint for his leg. While the man put on the splint, the stranger recounted his story.

"We took gold from the owner of a large hacienda. When the federal troops came, our band broke up and we all went off in different directions. I had the misfortune to fall off my horse and break my leg."

The stranger had finished his story by the time the man had put on the splint. The stranger, who was now able to mount his horse, thanked the man.

"After I leave, you go and look inside that tree," he said, pointing to a large mesquite nearby.

When the stranger was far from sight, the poor man ran to the tree. He looked inside and found a leather pouch full of gold coins. The man had never seen so much money in his entire life.

"What shall I do?" he wondered.

He was so excited that he forgot all about his hunger and weariness. Finally, he decided to ask the patron for advice.

He ran all the way back to the ranch and entered the patron's house with his hat in his hand.

"Who can the money rightfully belong to?" he asked. "Maybe we can get a reward."

The patron, who through great cunning had attained that rank, quickly analyzed the situation. He convinced the excited peasant, who felt honored just being inside the great man's house, that it was important to keep his adventure a secret. He then asked one of the servants to prepare some food for the confused man. When the man had eaten, the patron told him to go home.

"I'll take care of everything," he said.

The man finally made his way home.

"Where have you been?" asked his wife. "Did you have any luck today?"

The man did not mention what had happened. The rest of the evening whirled by like a sandstorm and that night he went to bed dreaming about the reward he would soon receive.

The man waited and waited for the patron to come and tell him what had developed. Several days went by and still he had received no news. Finally, he got up his courage and went to see the patron.

"What kind of reward did we get?" he asked.

The patron told him to wait, and went inside the house. The poor man was so anxious he could hardly stand still. When the patron came out, he had a large rope in his hands.

"Here, this is your reward," he said.

"What can I do with this rope?" asked the man. "I don't have any cows or horses."

The patron said, "See that poplar tree? This is for you to go and hang yourself, for being such a fool."

A Fiendish Compadre
Gets Caught

THERE were two compadres, one a muleteer and
the other a bandit. The muleteer journeyed from
Mexico City up north to Chihuahua and stopped
off at his compadre's house whenever he happened to
be in the area. The bandit had a little boy and the muleteer had baptized him. He brought him presents and
gave him money every time he saw him. The muleteer
visited his compadre's house with great confidence, felt
right at home, and enjoyed his visits immensely.

The mule driver had been away for six months and
was on his way back from Chihuahua with his mules
laden with silver. He had a little dog that he carried
between the bags on the mules' backs.

When he got to his compadre's house, they exchanged

warm greetings and everyone settled down for a comfortable evening. After a fine dinner, they all went outside to look at the stars and sit next to the fire. They had many stories to tell each other about their adventures and the conversation and laughter lasted long into the night.

In the morning, while the muleteer was still asleep, the bandit was doing his chores and happened upon a half-open bag of silver. As soon as he saw the money, greedy thoughts started going through his head and he ran to tell the other members of his gang what he had seen.

"All right, boys, we're going to follow my compadre when he leaves here today," he told them.

That afternoon, after getting the mules packed and saying good-bye to his godson and his friends, the mule driver started out. When it began getting dark, he stopped at a clearing where muleteers often spent the night. He made camp a short distance from the main section, built a fire, and ate his supper.

All during the day, the bandit had been following his compadre at some distance so as not to be seen. He and his men now hid in the bushes nearby, waiting for a chance to attack him.

The muleteer finally dozed off to sleep, but was awakened by the loud barking of his dog.

"Keep quiet and go to sleep," he told the dog. "You're going to wake the whole camp." However, as soon as the muleteer put his head down, the dog started barking again and running frantically back and forth.

"What's wrong with this crazy dog?" the muleteer wondered.

The bandit, who was at the head of his pack, started dragging himself along the ground. He wanted to catch his compadre by surprise. Every time the bandit stopped, the little dog would stop barking, and every time he started moving, the dog would begin to bark again.

The muleteer finally realized that something was wrong, took out his rifle, and started looking around. Every now and then the dog would stop running and, ears pointing straight up, would peer into the night. One time, when the dog stopped to look, the mule driver sighted his rifle between the dog's ears and fired. The shot resounded in the calm night and he heard the sound of feet running away. The little dog stopped barking and they both went to sleep.

Early the next morning, the driver got his mules ready to leave and placed the dog on top of one of them. He then decided to go and look at the place where he had heard the noise during the night. He thought it might have been an animal and was curious to see what kind of tracks he would find.

The first thing he saw when he got there was his compadre, the bandit, lying on the ground with a bullet hole in the middle of his forehead. The muleteer became very sad and thought of all the presents and money he had given his compadre.

"Even so, he tried to kill me," he said to his dog.

After a while he went to get his mules and started on his way again.

A Lesson From
A Lovelorn Cow

THERE once lived a man who was extremely jealous of his wife. She could do almost nothing without fear of arousing his suspicion. She was even afraid to look around when they were walking down the street because her husband might think she was looking at another man.

The couple had gotten married in La Encarnación de Diaz. Since none of the couple's relatives were very wealthy, their wedding had been rather modest. After the church ceremony, they had all gone back to Santa María where their friends had arranged for some of the local musicians to provide entertainment.

Everyone was having such a good time that they didn't notice Don Ricardo, the son of a wealthy ranchero, ride up on his horse. He went up to where the people were dancing and got off his horse. Don Ricardo, who had a sharp eye for the ladies, quickly spotted the newlyweds and asked the bride for a dance. The husband could not refuse since it was traditional for the bride to dance with the guests on her wedding day.

Later that evening, when the couple was alone, the groom kept berating his wife. "How did it feel, dancing with a rich man?" he shouted. His wife, who had had a wonderful day, was soon in tears. She could not understand why her husband was so jealous. As far as she was concerned, she had done nothing wrong.

Some months later, while out on a walk, the couple passed Don Ricardo on the road. "Good day, Señora," he said to the wife, completely ignoring the husband. The wife, who now knew how jealous her husband was, turned her head as if she had not seen him. But her husband began berating her as soon as Don Ricardo had gone away.

"Pack all your things this evening," he shouted. "We're going to leave this ranch in the morning."

The next morning they left. They moved away to a small village about three days ride to the north. They found a little house to rent and the wife settled down to the business of keeping house. Her husband found a job making adobe bricks and seemed quite content. After they had lived there for a few months, the husband had even made enough money to buy a cow.

"Now we will have all the milk we can drink," he proudly told his wife.

Indeed, this cow was to play a very important role in the marriage. But this waits to be seen.

In the meantime, the cow met a charming bull and fell deeply in love. The two animals were inseparable. One day, as they walked along the stream, the bull unexpectedly proposed to the cow.

"I don't know," she told the bull. "My master is a very jealous man and we might move away at any moment. If we were betrothed, this would break my heart."

The bull assured her that everything would turn out all right.

About this time a candy vendor began passing up their street regularly. He was an extremely handsome youth and the wife often bought candy from him. One evening, as her husband was coming home from work, he saw them conversing on the street corner.

"I can't even go to work without you flirting," he scolded her. "How long have you been seeing him?"

The wife, who had always been loyal to her husband, had only talked to the young man a few times. But her husband's extreme jealousy had eaten away at her patience and that evening they had an exhausting fight. She told him that his jealousy was making her life miserable, that neither of them would be happy as long as he was so suspicious. He told her that he didn't trust her and that he never had.

"Will I ever find peace of mind?" he shouted. That evening he decided to quit his job and move again.

Two days later the couple was up at dawn and preparing to leave. The wife had been very reluctant, but had finally decided to go with her husband. The burro was loaded with their belongings, the cow was harnessed, and the four of them started on their way.

They had traveled only a few miles when the cow began to moo.

"What's wrong with that infernal cow?" shouted the husband.

His wife told him about the love affair between the cow and the bull. She told him how they had been inseparable since they first met. The man shrugged his shoulders and asked his wife to calm the cow down. The cow was finally quieted and they continued on their journey.

After a few more miles the cow began to moo again. The wife again calmed her down. In this manner they proceeded for the rest of the day.

That evening they camped by the side of the road. By this time the cow's bellowing could be heard for miles. The husband had developed a bad headache and was very irritated.

"Would you please shut that cow up before I kill her," he yelled.

The woman was very scared and went to where the cow was tied. "Shut up your mouth, idiot," she scolded the cow. "Won't there be other bulls where we're going?"

The man, who was sitting dejectedly against a mesquite, overheard his wife and began to contemplate. "Won't there be other bulls where we are going?" This phrase stuck in his mind and he couldn't get rid of it. He finally got into his blankets and fell asleep.

What a dream he must have had because his whole attitude changed overnight. The couple turned around and started back home the very next morning. When they got back, the man returned to his old job. His wife, who soon became pregnant, was overjoyed at the turn of events. And the cow and the bull, as they richly deserved, lived happily ever after.

A Tale of Love

IT was that time when the swallows return. They leave on the feast day of San José and come back on the feast day of San Juan. They say that many cross the ocean but few return, because they are eaten by the Moors.

They waste no time, once on land, but begin immediately to gather mud and build their nests. Most of them choose the eaves of houses and barns, but one young and especially pretty swallow chose the belfry of a little church.

In the churchyard there was a large mesquite tree where a pitacochi came and sang every day. One morning, when the swallow stuck her neck out to hear better, he noticed her and began to sing as he had never sung before. It was truly love at first sight.

From then on the two birds spent every moment together. In the mornings, they would circle low around the village and then fly away into the countryside. And in the evenings, they would rest on the branches of the mesquite and he would serenade her. Indeed, the little swallow made a wonderful summer for the pitacochi.

Time flew by and the green leaves turned to gold. One day, as they sat on a branch of the mesquite, the pitacochi noticed how sad the swallow's eyes were and how she bent her head.

"What's the matter?" the pitacochi asked. "Why are you so sad?"

The little swallow was silent for a moment, then looked up at him. "The time for us to leave is almost here and I wish I didn't have to go. It will hurt me to leave you," she said, bending her head down again.

"That's right," said the pitacochi. "I'm so in love that I had forgotten you have to leave." The pitacochi tried to comfort her. "You can stay here with me. I'll take care of you."

The swallow looked up at him again. "We must all go away together," she told him. "If I stay here, I will surely die."

"Then I'll go with you," said the pitacochi.

Though his decision made the little swallow happy, she still tried to change his mind. "You'll never make it," she said. "We have to fly clear across the ocean and you're too heavy." But despite all her pleading, the pitacochi was determined to go with her.

Swallows always carry two small twigs in their beaks, when they fly over the sea, so they can rest on the waves when they become tired. And so, when the

128

feast day of San José arrived, the swallow had two little twigs ready for the pitacochi. When they reached the edge of the sea, they stopped on a cliff top to rest, and once more the swallow tried to persuade the pitacochi to change his mind.

"It's best for you to remain here," she said. "If you should have to turn back, I'll never stop worrying about you."

In the distance the flock made crooked little lines against the blue horizon.

"You wait here," said the swallow, "and if God grants, I'll return and we'll be together again."

The pitacochi looked out at the mighty sea. "We'd better catch up with the rest," he said.

The land kept sinking deeper each time the swallow turned around. "Drop your twigs in the water," she would tell the pitacochi when she noticed him getting tired. They would stop to rest for awhile and then start up again. But after many tries, the pitacochi lost all hope.

"You're right," he cried. "I cannot make it. I'm not good for anything. I wish I were dead."

He tried to make the swallow catch up with the flock.

"We're not too far out yet," he said. "You must go on."

"No," said the swallow. "If I let you go back alone, I will surely die of grief."

The two birds slowly made their way back to shore. When they were on the cliff top once again, they began to weep.

"Wait for me," the swallow told the pitacochi, "and pray to God that I can return."

They embraced each other for the last time and the little swallow spread her wings and took off. "Adiós," she called as she swooped out toward the sea.

The pitacochi stood on the cliff watching, with tears rolling from his eyes, until he could no longer see the fading form of his love.

Summer came once more and it was time again for the swallows to return. When they arrived, they began as usual to build their nests in the eaves of houses and barns. The pitacochi waited and waited for the little swallow to return. But he was still sitting alone in the mesquite tree when the stars came out that evening.

And so it was every summer until one day, he waited no more.

Two Sisters and a Harlot

THERE once lived two young sisters of very wealthy means who were renowned for their chastity. Across the street from them lived a beautiful woman, by nature a harlot, who was very popular with the men of the town. The two sisters spent much of their day gaping at the incessant procession that came and went from the woman's house and excoriating the woman.

One day, as they stood by the window, one of the sisters said, "I'm going to buy a jar and a bag of beans to keep track of the number of men who enter."

The sisters left the house through the back entrance and walked to the marketplace. When they returned, they placed a jar on a table beside the window and sat on either side of the table. For every man who entered the harlot's house, they tossed a bean in the jar.

Time passed and the jar began to overflow.

One day, as they sat tossing beans as usual, one of the sisters became ill. She was taken up to her room immediately and a physician was summoned to her bedside. But despite all his remedies, her fever raged, and by morning the news was spread that the girl lay dying.

By midday, everyone except the florist and the woman across the street had paid the girl a visit. The mourners came and went, lamenting her being taken in the prime of her youth but consoling themselves with her goodness and saintliness.

From her doorway, the woman of the street could hear the mourning and see the beautiful flowers that everyone brought. It being that the idle worms were growing in her fingers that day, she decided to walk across the street and pay her respects also. "Maybe the poor child will ask God to forgive my wickedness," she thought.

There was great astonishment when the woman appeared at the door. Everyone turned scornful faces to her and wouldn't permit her inside. However, she was insistent and made her way through the milling throng to the deathbed.

The dying girl became hysterical when she saw the woman. "Dios mío, Dios mío, get that wicked woman out of my sight," she screamed.

The woman was so ashamed that she bent her head and disappeared into the crowd. But instead of leaving the house, she fell to her knees and crawled into an empty room where she collapsed behind a bed and died.

There was much weeping and wailing when the sister passed away later that evening. "Such a wonderful girl," the people cried. "She is surely at the right hand of God." They brought more bouquets than ever and placed them at her bedside.

But soon after the girl's death, something strange and unwonted began to occur. The flowers started to vanish as soon as they were placed beside her body. The mourners became very frightened and recalled the priest to the girl's bedside, imploring him to ask the girl why she refused the flowers.

"Was it because she is already in heaven and has no use for them?" they asked.

The priest bent over the dead girl. "You who were so good on this earth," he asked, "why do you refuse the flowers that are offered?"

There was a pause and then the girl answered. "Father, you will find the flowers in the room down the hall," she said. "The woman there is the one who deserves them." Then she went on. "There are two requests I make of you. Don't bury my body in holy ground. And please tell my sister to throw away the jar of beans."

After this, the girl was silent.

When the people opened the door to the room down the hall, a profusion of flowers came pouring down upon them. It was not until the room had been emptied of flowers that they found the poor harlot lying behind the bed.

The Sabio Sees a Sow

THERE was a man living in Santa María who was reputed to have the gift of divination. Everyone thought he had the ability to find things that had been lost.

Actually, he had been deceiving the people for a long time by taking things from their houses, hiding them for awhile, then pretending to retrieve them with the help of his uncanny powers. His reputation grew and grew until his fame had spread throughout the region.

"There goes the sabio*," the people would exclaim whenever he passed.

One day, a group of pistoleros came down to the fair from a rancho called Los Rosanos. This rancho was

---

*Seer.

notorious for its bad men and bandits. They went to Porfirio's cantina and started drinking. After some general conversation they began to talk about the sabio. Some believed he really had the power of divination while others thought he was an imposter. Finally, when the conversation degenerated into an argument, someone suggested killing a pig and burying it behind the cantina. In this manner, the power of the sabio would be tested.

Early the next morning, the group of outlaws went to the sabio's house and woke him up with loud knocking.

"Who is it?" the sabio called through the window.

The men replied, "Something has been buried behind Porfirio's cantina. Since you are a sabio, come and tell us what is buried there."

The sleepy sabio was reluctant to get out of bed, but he recognized the men and decided that it would not be wise to oppose their wishes. "The devil's really got hold of me now," he thought as he walked with them toward the cantina.

Word had gotten around quickly and there was a large crowd of people waiting for the sabio to arrive. As soon as he got there, they began to ask him questions. They all wanted to know what was buried behind the cantina.

"Give me time to think it over," replied the sabio. "Sometimes the spirits take a long time to answer."

Three days went by and the sabio had still not given his answer. The people started to get angry.

"What's buried inside?" they shouted at the frightened man. "You have been allowed more than enough time. Give us your answer."

The poor sabio was very frightened and didn't know what to do. "I might as well tell them the truth," he decided. Everyone watched attentively as he walked toward the back of the cantina.

"This is it," he said dejectedly. "This is where the sow twisted her tail."

This was his way of admitting that he had finally been discovered as a fake. But as soon as the bandits heard the word "sow," they exploded in cheers. Soon everyone was shouting, "Que viva el Sabio! Que viva el Sabio!"

Needless to say, our hero had had such a fright that he never wanted to practice divination again. He preferred to lose his reputation rather than his life.